One-Minute History Lessons

Six Millennia of
Great Jewish Leaders

TARGUM/FELDHEIM

First published 2003
Copyright © 2003 by Moshe Goldberger
P.O. Box 82
Staten Island, NY 10309
ISBN 1-56871-238-3

Published by:
TARGUM PRESS, INC.
22700 W. Eleven Mile Rd.
Southfield, MI 48034
E-mail: targum@netvision.net.il
Fax: 888-298-9992
www.targum.com

Distributed by:
FELDHEIM PUBLISHERS
202 Airport Executive Park
Nanuet, NY 10954

Printed in Israel

In honor of our children,

Sarah, Molly, and Joshua

Arlynn and Daniel Bock

With thanks to:

Yitzchak E. Gold
Rabbi Eliezer Gevirtz
Rabbi Menachem Goldman
Rabbi Mordechai Gelber
Binyamin Siegel
Charles Mamiye
Mordechai Kairey
Daniel Bock
Daniel Lemberg
and others

Contents

Part 8: *Acharonim*

Introduction

The main focus of the Torah is to provide us with Hashem's program for how to succeed in life. For this reason, the Torah not only contains the mitzvos but also relates countless incidents from the lives of our great leaders. From the events that happened in the past and the deeds our ancestors performed we learn how to improve ourselves and meet the challenges sent our way.

We can learn countless historical lessons from the Torah and from our leaders. In this work, through our "one-minute history lessons," we will be summarizing many of these lessons. Our goal is to understand history through the eyes of the Torah Sages, as well as to gain insight from their personal greatness.

To meet this goal, we have divided the book into seven sections. Part 1, "Foundation of the World," focuses on lessons to be learned from the early years of world history. The leaders of the time, Adam, Sheis, and Noach, achieved levels far beyond our comprehension. On the other hand, the failures of the people of their time teach us important lessons about Hashem's system of reward and punishment. We also learn about the *avos*, Avraham, Yitzchak, and Yaakov, who are the great founders of our nation.

Part 2, "Early Years of Our Nation," touches on the main events of the establishment of *klal Yisrael* — the slavery in Egypt, the leadership of Moshe, the reign of the judges, and the kingship of David and Shlomo. Due to the lack of time and space, these ideas could not be developed fully, since that would necessitate an in-depth study of Tanach and would result in a historical encyclopedia, which is not the goal of this book. We give a few lessons from the major events of these years.

Part 3, "Kings and Prophets," begins with the split of the Jewish people into two separate kingdoms. Lessons learned from the kings and prophets of this era and from the Babylonian exile are briefly reviewed.

Starting from Part 4, "Age of the *Tannaim*," we focus on the leaders of our nation rather than on the events that occurred. Developing an appreciation for our leaders is the first step in understanding who we are as a people and what we have accomplished over time. In each generation, Hashem sends Jewry the leaders we need to help us grow.

The last three sections of the book, "Later Leaders in Babylonia," "*Rishonim*," and "*Acharonim*," provide glimpses into the lives of great Torah scholars and spiritual giants who have taught *klal Yisrael* for the last thousand years. We have attempted to cover a broad scope of Torah leaders and gain insight from their actions and writings. Of course, it is impossible to discuss every *gadol* (Torah leader), and we have been forced to omit many either for space considerations or because their influence is not as easy to perceive. We hope our readers will gain much from the lessons presented in this book and utilize them as starting points to learning more about each era.

The Challenge of Writing on History

It is difficult to write an accurate, objective, concise book of history. Imagine three different people, one a close follower of Rav Moshe Feinstein, *zt"l*, one a close follower of Rav Yaakov Kamenetsky, *zt"l*, and one a close follower of the Satmar Rebbe, *zt"l*, telling us their perspective of the history of the last generation. Each disciple will have a different way of looking at the events of that generation.

Every one of us views history subjectively, based on our background and worldviews. In this book, we will attempt, with Hashem's help, to focus on clear facts and to document the sources so that we can clarify the Torah's perspective on history. The insights of our sages in every generation help us appreciate the events and people who came before us.

Our general approach is based on the teachings of Rav Avigdor Miller, *zt"l*, which have been preserved to a large extent in his books and tapes. Many of the dates in this book are based on the dates Rav Miller uses. These dates are not intended as authoritative, but hold true within a small range of time.

Please note: We are not attempting to portray the full history of the Jewish people. The goal of this work is to extract some lessons from our glorious past in order to reach our potential in the present. We are also not attempting to describe every facet of the great personalities discussed in the following pages. Each of these spiritual giants deserves many volumes dedicated to his individual history, and some have already been written. We are only trying to give the reader a taste of the lessons to be learned from these sublime servants of Hashem, to lead the reader to pursue more of the books and *sefarim* that are available about these Torah giants.

Additional note: The year 5764 (the year of this book's first printing) corresponds to the non-Jewish years of 2003–4. We refer to these 2004 years as the "Common Era," or "C.E." In this work, we use the Jewish year to refer to events in Jewish history, which begins with the creation of the world. In order to relate more easily to the later dates in history, we also include references to the Gregorian calendar for those years.

(The actual first year of the Common Era is open to discussion. For details see *Am Olam: The History of the Eternal Nation*, by Rav Shlomo Rotenberg, pg. 77, which quotes a number of non-Jewish sources on this subject.)

Part 1

Foundation of the World

Chapter 1

The Beginning

History begins with Adam, the first man, who was created by Hashem on the sixth day of Creation. The creation of man was the culmination of the six days of Creation. But unlike animals and plants, which came into existence all over the world at once (*Chullin* 60a), man was created singular and alone, so that each person should say, "Because of me, Hashem created the entire universe" (*Sanhedrin* 37a).

Adam was created in the fifth hour of the first Friday. His wife, Chavah, was created in the seventh hour of the day, and in the eighth hour Chavah gave birth to Kayin and his twin sister (*Sanhedrin* 38b).

Adam lived 930 years. Thus, he was able to see the nine generations that followed him, including Lemech, who was Noach's father.

One-minute history lesson: The Mishnah teaches, "The world was created with ten sayings..." (*Avos* 5:1). Why did Hashem create the world with ten statements when He could have easily done it with just one?

The reason is explained in the Mishnah. The ten statements used in the creation of the world signify the importance of the universe. The wicked are more accountable for destroying Hashem's world and the righteous are more worthy of abundant rewards. This obligates us to be responsible for our words and deeds during our lifetimes in this world.

Chapter 2

Patience

The Torah devotes many verses to listing the ten generations from Adam to Noach. We learn their names, at what age their children were born, and when they died.

What is the significance of this information?

This teaches us the extent of Hashem's patience. Hashem refrained from punishing the sinners of those generations for many years, allowing them time to repent, until He eventually brought the great flood in the year 1656 (*Avos* 5:2–3).

Among these ten generations, we do have three outstanding leaders, who are listed among the seven great leaders of old: Adam, Sheis, and Mesushelach (*Sukkah* 52b). We are taught that Adam was a very pious person. He fasted to achieve atonement for his one sin for 130 years (*Eiruvin* 18b). Sheis, his son, was just like his father and was successful in all his ways (*Midrash Tehillim* 1:10). Mesushelach, a few generations later, was a complete tzaddik, who would always praise Hashem (*Yalkut Shimoni, Bereishis* 42).

One-minute history lesson: Hashem waited sixteen hundred and fifty-six years. What a lesson in patience! This is a practical lesson we can utilize in our daily lives. Next time you find yourself waiting ten minutes for something, remember this lesson: Hashem waited ten generations for Noach; surely I can wait ten minutes or even ten hours or ten days.

Why do we sometimes get angry at others for their seeming errors? We need to emulate the ways of Hashem and be more patient and forgiving.

Chapter 3

Reward and Punishment

*Three righteous people were the foundations of
the world: Adam, Noach, and Avraham.*
(*Midrash Tehillim* 34:1)

Noach lived for 950 years. It is noteworthy that
his three children were born after he was five
hundred years old (*Bereishis* 5:32). This "delay" was part of Hashem's plan so that Noach's three
children would still be worthy of being rescued with
their parents in the ark. Had Noach's three children
been born earlier, perhaps one or two of them would
have been corrupted by the people of that
generation.

The great flood lasted a year, from 17 Cheshvan,
1656, until 27 Cheshvan, 1657. Noach and his family were saved because Noach found favor in
Hashem's eyes (*Bereishis* 6:8), while all others were
destroyed because they had become corrupt.

To appreciate the greatness of these early leaders,
we need to keep in mind that they all studied and

observed the six universal laws which Hashem had instructed Adam: to avoid idolatry, blasphemy, bloodshed, immorality, and theft, as well as to teach and enforce all of these (See Rambam, *Hilchos Melachim* 9:1).

> *One-minute history lesson:* Throughout history this pattern is repeated: sooner or later the righteous are rewarded, while the wicked are punished. Entire civilizations have been wiped out by various means on account of their behavior. Hashem never overlooks wrongdoing, and He never fails to reward good deeds.

Chapter 4

Seventy Nations

After the great flood, Noach's three sons reacted differently to their father's indignity. Noach was granted a prophecy that Sheim, his most worthy son, would be the host of Hashem's Presence.

Later, the descendants of Noach's three sons developed into seventy nations: fourteen nations from Yefes, thirty nations from Cham, and twenty-six nations from Sheim (*Bereishis* 10:6–32).

When Yaakov's family came to Egypt later on, they were also seventy people (*Bereishis* 46:27). This parallel teaches us that Hashem considered each member of the Jewish people as equal to one of the nations of the world (*Devarim* 32:8).

> *One-minute history lesson:* Nothing in this world is a coincidence. Hashem is in complete control and arranges all of the details to correspond to each other.

Chapter 5

The Goal of Creation

There were ten generations from Noach until Avraham, which teaches us [again] the extent of Hashem's supreme patience, until Avraham Avinu came to receive the reward of all of them.
(*Avos* 5:3)

Avraham is called the Pillar of the World (Rambam, *Hilchos Avodah Zarah* 1:2). He began to establish the Jewish people as Hashem's children and taught them to listen to Hashem and live by His commandments. Hashem waited patiently 1,948 years (from the creation of the world) until Avraham was born.

Hashem had created a huge universe, but His goal in the creation was good people who would choose to follow His command.

One-minute history lesson: Hashem is waiting for each one of us to dedicate our lives to serving Hashem as Avraham Avinu did and justify

His creation. We need to proclaim, "I shall praise Your name forever" (*Tehillim* 145:2, which we say in *Ashrei* three times a day). The more we do for Hashem, the more we will be privileged to merit His reciprocation.

Chapter 6

The Righteous Unite

I n 1996 of the Jewish calendar, when Avraham was forty-eight years old, Hashem caused the Tower of Babel to be destroyed by the formation of many languages and dispersed the people to all parts of the world (*Bereishis* 11:9).

Until this point, everyone spoke the same language (ibid. 11:1), enabling them to unite for either positive or negative purposes.

> *When the righteous unite, it is a benefit to them and to the world.*
> (*Sanhedrin* 71b)

Hashem arranges for certain righteous individuals to meet for their mutual benefit and to help the world. Avraham was born in the year 1948 and Noach passed away in the year 2006. Thus, Avraham and Noach's lives overlapped for a period of fifty-eight years. In Hebrew, the numerical value of Noach's name (*nun* [50] + *ches* [8]) is fifty-eight.

This hints to the fifty-eight-year overlap in the lives of Avraham and Noach, intended by Hashem for Avraham to learn about Noach's great character and his experiences during the great flood and for Noach to learn from Avraham's brilliance and devotion to Hashem (*Seder Olam*).

As for those who were unworthy, Hashem decided to separate and scatter them — both for their benefit and to help the world (*Sanhedrin* 71b).

One-minute history lesson: The scattering of the nations highlights the teaching of the Mishnah in *Avos*: "Keep far away from bad neighbors and do not join with the wicked" (*Avos* 1:7).

Chapter 7

The World Plan

The Talmud (*Avodah Zarah* 9a) teaches us the big picture of Hashem's Plan for this world: Two thousand years of emptiness, two thousand years of Torah, and two thousand years of Mashiach's arrival.

We know that Hashem gave us the Torah at Mount Sinai in the year 2448 of the Jewish calendar. We also know that Avraham Avinu was born in 1948, five hundred years before the giving of the Torah. However, we just learned that the era of Torah began in the year 2000. The question arises: What took place in the year 2000 that is considered the beginning of the Torah era?

The Talmud (ibid.) answers this question by explaining that when Avraham was fifty-two years of age (in the year 2000), he embarked on a campaign to reach out and teach others the principles of belief in Hashem and the ways of righteousness. How did Avraham know the Torah five hundred years before it was given to the Jewish people? We are taught that he understood it on his own through his brilliant mind, his determination, and Divine inspiration (Rambam, *Hilchos Avodah Zarah* 1:3).

> *One-minute history lesson:* What a defining event! Although the Torah was not formally given to the Jewish people until the year 2448, we do not consider that year as the beginning of the Torah era. Rather, the beginning of the Torah era was Avraham Avinu's teaching of Torah to others. From this we learn how important it is to disseminate Torah to others as much as possible.
>
> The very first *Mishnah* in *Pirkei Avos* advises us, "Be cautious in judgment, teach many disciples, and make a fence for the Torah."

Chapter 8

Tests of Greatness

Avraham was more than just a righteous individual. Although there were other righteous people before him, such as Adam, Chanoch, Mesushelach, Noach, Sheim, and Ever, they were not chosen by Hashem for an everlasting covenant. Avraham was a supergiant among giants, "who fulfilled the Torah before it was given" (*Yoma* 28b).

Avraham was tested by Hashem time and time again, ten times (*Avos* 5:4), and he passed every test, demonstrating his overwhelming dedication to and love of Hashem.

These were Avraham's ten tests:

1. He was forced to hide for ten years as Nimrod sought to kill him.

2. He was thrown into a burning furnace by Nimrod.

3. Hashem made an eternal covenant with him, the *Bris Bein HaBesarim* and informed him of

the exile and affliction his children would endure for four hundred years.

4. At the age of seventy-five, he was instructed by Hashem to move away from his birthplace.

5. He had to leave Eretz Yisrael because of a famine.

6. His wife, Sarah, was abducted by Pharaoh.

7. He had to battle four kings in order to save his nephew, Lot.

8. When he was ninety-nine, he was instructed to circumcise himself and his thirteen-year-old son, Yishmael.

9. He was instructed to expel Yishmael and Hagar.

10. At the age of 137, he was instructed to offer his thirty-seven-year-old son, Yitzchak, as a sacrifice.

One-minute history lesson: Avraham's ten tests demonstrate his greatness. Our personal and national hero, Avraham is a super role model for success in life. We must always follow Avraham's ways and persevere in fulfilling Torah and mitzvos, even under adversity.

Chapter 9

Highlights of the Avos

Yitzchak was born in 2048, when Avraham was one hundred years old. He followed in the footsteps of his great parents, reaching the highest spiritual heights at age thirty-seven, when he consented to be offered as a sacrifice. After the *akeidah*, when Yitzchak's life was saved at the last minute, Yitzchak went on to live a life of perfection. He instituted *minchah*, the afternoon prayer and also taught the mitzvah of *maaser*, giving a tenth of one's assets to charity (*Rambam, Hilchos Melachim* 9:1).

Yaakov and Eisav were born in 2108, when Yitzchak was sixty years old (*Bereishis* 25:26). Although Eisav was the firstborn, Yaakov purchased the rights and privileges of the firstborn from him. Thus, at the age of sixty-three, Yaakov received the blessings from his father (ibid. 27:27–29).

Yaakov was known as an *ish tam* (a perfect or wholesome man) who followed in the ways of his father and grandfather and dedicated himself to Torah (*Bereishis* 25:27). He instituted *maariv*, the evening prayer (Rambam, *Hilchos Melachim* 9:1). All of his children were tzaddikim and merited to become the core of *klal Yisrael*, the *shivtei Kah*.

One-minute history lesson: Our Sages teach us that everything our three fathers did was a portent for the future. Their lives in general parallel three eras in history:

1. Avraham is the symbol of the era of the five *Chumashim* when the Jews were challenged by idolatry and Canaanite and Egyptian influences and received the Torah before entering Eretz Yisrael.

2. Yitzchak symbolized the 850 years from Yehoshua to the destruction of the first Beis HaMikdash, when the Jews lived in Eretz Yisrael, as Yitzchak did, in great prosperity and happiness.

3. Yaakov left Eretz Yisrael and went to Egypt, thus serving as a symbol of our exile among the nations (Rav A. Miller, *Behold a People*, p. 66).

Part 2

Early Years of Our Nation

Chapter 10

A New Era

In 2238, Yaakov Avinu, at age 130 (*Bereishis* 47:9), moved with his entire family of seventy individuals to Egypt. Yaakov's son Yosef had become second in command in that country nine years earlier. He saved the country from famine and held his position for eighty years, until 2309.

The Jews remained in Egypt until 2448, a total of 210 years. These were years of hardship and suffering. Egypt is called the "iron furnace" (*Devarim* 4:20) because that is where the Jewish people were forged into a nation. There they were purified and refined there to become worthy of receiving the Torah at Sinai (Rav Avigdor Miller, *A Nation Is Born*, p. 8). Hashem's first statement at Sinai was, "I am Hashem, your God, who took you out of the land of Egypt" (*Shemos* 20:2).

The Jewish nation was composed of 600,000 men between the ages of twenty and sixty and their families. Hashem redeemed them from slavery with ten astonishing miracles in Egypt and ten more miracles at the Reed Sea. The purpose of all these miracles was to teach us of Hashem's mastery over the universe and over us.

One-minute history lesson: We have a mitzvah to remember the Exodus at least twice daily (*Bemidbar* 15:40). Why is it so important? The Exodus from Egypt was a most defining milestone in our history: it made us into Hashem's chosen people forever!

Chapter 11

One Person Makes the Difference

Moshe Rabbeinu (our leader and teacher) was born in 2368. He led the Jewish nation out of Egypt in the year 2448, when he was eighty years old.

In that same year, the Jewish people received the Torah through Moshe Rabbeinu at Sinai. The Torah teaches that Moshe Rabbeinu was both the greatest prophet in history (*Devarim* 34:10) and the most humble person in history (*Bemidbar* 12:3).

Moshe was the one to confront Pharaoh and deliver the warnings of the Ten Plagues. At Hashem's command, he miraculously split the Yam Suf (the Reed Sea) on the seventh day after the Exodus. The miracle food, *mann*, fell in his merit the entire forty years that Moshe led the Jewish people in the desert.

Moshe went up Mount Sinai to accept the Torah

on our behalf, on Shabbos, the sixth day of Sivan, in the year 2448.

Moshe taught us the entire Torah and led the nation for forty years in the desert until he passed away at the age of 120, in the year 2488. The Revelation at Sinai was the most dramatic scene in the annals of world history. All Jews witnessed Hashem's presence on the mountaintop and heard Him teaching us the Ten Commandments. These ten laws encompass the entire Torah. Briefly, they are:

1. Hashem, our God, is the Creator and Controller of all.

2. There is no other god besides Him.

3. One must always respect Hashem's name.

4. One must observe the Shabbos.

5. One must honor his parents.

6. Do not murder.

7. Do not commit adultery.

8. Do not steal.

9. Do not bear false witness.

10. Do not covet that which belongs to others.

One-minute history lesson: The Rambam (*Hilchos Teshuvah* 5:2) teaches that we can all be as righteous as Moshe Rabbeinu. We all have great potential, and we all have the responsibility to develop ourselves to the fullest extent possible. Although we cannot match Moshe Rabbeinu's prophetic greatness, nor his humility, we are considered as righteous as he was when we achieve our potential.

Chapter 12

Yehoshua Shines

In 2488, Yehoshua led the Jewish nation into Eretz Yisrael. As Moshe's greatest disciple, he transmitted the Torah from Moshe to all of the Elders who led the nation afterward (*Avos* 1:1). Moshe Rabbeinu is compared to the sun, while Yehoshua is compared to the moon, which reflects the sun's light (*Bava Basra* 5a).

It took seven years to conquer the land, and seven more years to divide the land. During these years, the Mishkan, the Tabernacle that had been erected in the desert, was in Gilgal. In 2503, a permanent structure for the Mishkan was built in Shiloh, where the Mishkan stood for 369 years (*Zevachim* 118b).

Yehoshua was the leader of the Jewish nation for twenty-eight years, until he passed away in the year 2516. His great success was a result of his total dedication to Torah study, as we see from his encounter with an angel before the battle with Yericho

(*Yehoshua*, ch. 5). Rabbi Akiva Eiger, in his notes on the Talmud (on *Shabbos* 55b), quotes a source that lists Yehoshua as one of those who died only as a result of the serpent that caused Adam's sin.

Yehoshua wrote his *sefer* of Tanach (*Bava Basra* 14b), and if Jews had not sinned the Torah would have remained only the five books of Moshe and *Sefer Yehoshua* (*Nedarim* 22b).

One-minute history lesson: Many miraculous events occurred during the years that Yehoshua led the people. The fact that *Bnei Yisrael* succeeded in conquering the seven powerful nations living in the land was the greatest and most obvious miracle of all. Through the many miracles that are described in Tanach, we see the obvious hand of Hashem controlling history.

Why were the seven nations inhabiting Eretz Yisrael up until that time cast out from the land? The Gemara (*Bava Kama* 38a) teaches that they transgressed the "Seven Laws of Noach" which are required of every human being. We are taught that Eretz Yisrael cannot tolerate those who transgress the mitzvos, which is why even we are punished with exile if we do not fulfill Torah and mitzvos.

Chapter 13

Righteous Leaders

After the death of Yehoshua, the Jewish people were led by the Elders, beginning with Kalev ben Yefuneh, who led for seventeen years, from 2516 to 2533.

In 2533, Osniel ben Kenaz, a son-in-law of Kalev, became the first judge. He ruled for forty years (*Shoftim* 3:11). His name signifies that Hashem answered him (*Temurah* 16a). The Midrash records that he was considered great enough to replace Yehoshua (*Bereishis Rabbah* 58:2).

Beginning from 2573, Eihud judged for eighty years (*Shoftim* 3:30).

Beginning from 2654, Devorah and Barak judged for forty years. Devorah was one of seven prophetesses in Jewish history (*Megillah* 14a). Her famous song, *Shiras Devorah*, is one of the ten great songs of our history. The Midrash relates that she made her husband great by producing thick wicks that she had him deliver to the Mishkan in Shiloh. She would sit under a palm tree to judge the people to avoid *yichud* (seclusion with men).

Beginning from 2694, Gideon (Yerubaal) judged for forty years. Because he praised the Jewish nation, he was empowered to save them (*Shoftim* 6:14).

Beginning from 2736, Tola ruled for twenty-three years.

Beginning from 2758, Yair ruled for twenty-two years.

Beginning from 2779, Yiftach ruled for six years.

Beginning from 2785, Ivtzan (Boaz) ruled for seven years. He and his *beis din* (judicial court) instituted that people should greet each other with Hashem's name, and the Heavenly *Beis Din* consented to this ruling (*Makkos* 23b). He later married Rus, who gave birth to Oveid, grandfather of David.

Beginning from 2810, the mighty Shimshon ruled for twenty years. The Gemara tells us, "He judged the Jewish nation as [fairly as] their Father in Heaven" (*Sotah* 10a and *Rashi*). Shimshon's physical strength was a singularly unique blessing from Hashem. It is compared to that of the giant Goliath.

One-minute history lesson: "There was at least one judge from each of the twelve tribes.... There was at least one prophet from each of the tribes" (*Sukkah* 27b).

Hashem demonstrates in history that opportunities for greatness are open to all. No matter which tribe one was from, one had the opportunity to become a great judge or prophet.

For more information on the judges, see *Behold a People*, by Rav Avigdor Miller, *zt"l* (New York, 1968), which teaches how to appreciate and emulate these great giants, and *Samson's Struggle* by Rabbi Gershon Weiss, *shlita* (New York: Feldheim Publishers, 1989), which teaches the life and legacy of Shimshon.

Chapter 14

Shmuel the Prophet

Beginning from 2830, Eili, the *kohein gadol* (high priest), ruled as a judge for forty years (*Shmuel* I 4:18). Because Eili's sons did not follow in their father's ways to the level that was expected of them, they were killed in battle and the Mishkan was captured by the Pelishtim. The Talmud (*Shabbos* 55b) says it is a mistake to think that they sinned in the serious manner that is described in the text. It was decreed that Eili's descendants would die young unless they engaged in Torah study and acts of kindness (*Rosh HaShanah* 18a).

Eili's disciple, Shmuel, began his career as the last of the judges and the first of the major prophets of this era in 2871. He is considered the teacher of all the prophets (*Yerushalmi Chagigah* 2:1). In addition, he is compared to Moshe Rabbeinu and Aharon HaKohein (see *Tehillim* 99:6). He wrote the books of *Shoftim*, *Shmuel*, and *Rus* (*Bava Basra* 14b, *Rashi*).

Shmuel's father, Elkanah, was an extraordinary

tzaddik, unique in his generation. Shmuel's mother, Chanah, was one of the seven prophetesses mentioned in Tanach (*Megillah* 14a).

Shmuel was instructed by Hashem to anoint Shaul as the first Jewish king. A few years later, the kingship was taken from Shaul and Hashem had Shmuel anoint David.

David became king at the age of thirty in 2883. For the first seven years of his reign, David ruled over Yehudah in Chevron. Then he established his throne in Yerushalayim, where he ruled over the entire nation for the remaining thirty-three years of his life.

One-minute history lesson: Although David was the youngest of his brothers, Hashem chose him as king because he had perfected his character to the greatest extent. Hashem can choose you, too, if you do your part. The door is open for each individual to develop his character, increase his Torah knowledge, and serve Hashem more.

Chapter 15

David's Challenges

Although David was informed by the Prophet Shmuel that he was to be the new king, it was initially kept a secret from the people. David, the chosen one, was then accused unjustly of being in competition with King Shaul and was persecuted by him. Later in life, he faced rebellions and battles. He was forced to flee for his life, time and time again, yet his love for and trust in Hashem never wavered.

David utilized his sufferings to compose *sefer Tehillim*, which became one of the twenty-four books of Tanach. Many of our prayers in the siddur come from *Tehillim*, and all types of private prayers can be found there, too. The Midrash *Shochar Tov* notes that *sefer Tehillim* is divided into five books, parallel to the five books of the Torah. It contains psalms by nine other historical leaders, including Adam, Sheim, Avraham Avinu, and Moshe Rabbeinu (*Bava Basra* 14b).

Why did our ancestors suffer from childlessness?
Because Hashem desires the prayers of the
righteous.
(*Yevamos* 64a)

One-minute history lesson: Every problem in life can be utilized in a positive way. As we learn in *Mishlei*, "A tzaddik falls seven times, but he keeps on rising" (*Mishlei* 24:16).

Chapter 16

David's Building

David wanted to build the Beis HaMikdash, the Holy Temple, and he made all the necessary preparations for the building that his son Shlomo eventually built.

The goal of the Beis HaMikdash was to express our gratitude to Hashem by housing the Ark, containing the Stone Tablets, in a permanent structure. The *Shechinah* (Hashem's Presence) resided there, making it the ideal place for prayer and sacrifices (Rav Avigdor Miller, *Behold a People*, p. 429).

The Rambam teaches that the location of the *mizbei'ach* (altar) in the Beis HaMikdash is the place where Yitzchak was bound by his father at the *akeidah*, where Noach brought his offerings after the great flood, where Kayin and Hevel (Cain and Abel) brought their offerings, and where Adam, the first human, brought his offering. It is also the spot from where Hashem took the earth for the creation of Adam (*Hilchos Beis HaBechirah* 2:1–2).

One-minute history lesson: From this series of connected events, we see that history is not a collection of random happenings. Hashem keeps track of everything we do and when and how we do it. Like our forefathers, we can invest a place with holiness if we so choose.

Chapter 17

Shlomo's Success

In 2924, Shlomo HaMelech became king at the age of twelve when his father David passed away (*Melachim* I 2:12).

Four years later, Shlomo began to build the First Beis HaMikdash, the First Temple. This was 480 years after the Jews left Egypt (ibid. 6:1). This edifice became "Hashem's dwelling forever, the place He desires" (*Tehillim* 132:14).

At the beginning of his reign, Shlomo was offered a gift from Hashem. He requested "an understanding heart to judge the nation" (*Melachim* I 3:9). Hashem was so pleased with this request that He not only granted him wisdom but also gave him long life, wealth, and victory over his enemies.

Shlomo gave us *Sefer Mishlei* (Proverbs), *Shir HaShirim* (Song of Songs), and *Koheles* (Ecclesiastes). These three *sefarim* teach us who Shlomo HaMelech was and how he lived. He was a master of wisdom, self-control, and love of Hashem.

Shlomo was one of our greatest teachers, on whose behalf Hashem continues to bless us. When we say special prayers in the synagogue for the sick, a "*Mi Shebeirach*," we mention, "He Who has blessed our fathers, Avraham, Yitzchak, and Yaakov, Moshe, Aharon, David, and Shlomo...."

One-minute history lesson: The following are some of the many lessons we learn from Shlomo HaMelech's *sefarim*:

- "One who has a good attitude will always be happy" (*Mishlei* 15:15).

- "A gentle response will turn away anger" (ibid., 1).

- "One who guards his mouth and tongue will be saved from many troubles" (ibid. 21:23).

Part 3

Kings and Prophets

Chapter 18

The Split

When Rechavam, son of Shlomo, took over the kingship in 2964, most of the Jewish nation decided to follow Yarovam ben Nevat of the Tribe of Ephraim, who established a new kingdom in Shechem. Only the tribes of Yehudah and Binyamin remained with Rechavam in Yerushalayim.

There are many lessons to be learned from this tragic division of the nation. The prophet teaches us that Rechavam refused to accept the advice of the Elders, who counseled that he negotiate with the people with humility (*Melachim* I 12:8).

Yarovam, too, made mistakes. Although at first he was a righteous person, he decided to avoid coming to the Beis HaMikdash, knowing he would have to submit himself before the kings of the House of David. This eventually caused his downfall (*Sanhedrin* 102a).

One-minute history lesson: A person can only succeed as a leader if he is humble and willing to listen to others. Failure to submit and to take advice can lead to losing one's power, like Rechavam, or losing one's share in the World to Come, as did Yarovam.

Chapter 19

The Following Generations

Rechavam, Shlomo's son, ruled for seventeen years, beginning in 2964.

Aviyah, his son, ruled for three years.

Asa, his son, ruled for forty-one years, following the ways of Hashem (*Melachim* I 15:10.) He cleared away all idolatry from Eretz Yisrael (*Shabbos* 56b). He pursued his enemies with trust in Hashem and won. He was an exceptional tzaddik (*Sotah* 10a), but when he utilized Torah scholars to build cities, he was punished with a foot ailment.

The kingdom of the Ten Tribes, Yisrael, did not fair so well. Yarovam, also beginning in the year 2964, ruled for twenty-two years. At first, he also was a great Torah scholar (*Sanhedrin* 10a), but he sinned in rebuking Shlomo HaMelech in public. Once he became king, he sinned by building golden calves and causing others to sin (*Avos* 5:21).

Nadav, his son, ruled for two years, also in wickedness.

Nadav was attacked by Basha ben Achiyah, who destroyed Yarovam's family and ruled over Yisrael for twenty-four years, also in wickedness.

Eilah, his son, ruled for two years, in wickedness.

Zimri, his subject, took over for seven days, followed by Omri, who ruled for twelve years.

One-minute history lesson: The breakaway group, the Ten Tribes, began to deteriorate gradually until they were finally exiled among the nations. As we learned in the previous chapter, this began with the failure to listen to the advice of the Elders, as the Talmud teaches, "If elders advise you to demolish and young advisors encourage you to build, demolish and don't build because the demolishing of elders will result in building whereas the building of youth is demolishing" (*Megillah* 31b). Let us take this as a lesson for ourselves, too. We need to always live by the maxim "Accept upon yourself a rabbinic authority" (*Avos* 1:16).

Chapter 20

Hashem's Response

In 3024, Yehoshafat, son of Asa, began his twenty-five-year reign over Yehudah (*Melachim* I 22:42). He honored Torah scholars greatly (*Kesubos* 103b), and he would win wars by singing praises to Hashem.

Parallel to him in Yisrael was Achav, son of Omri, who began his twenty-two-year reign in 3021 (*Melachim* I 16:29–30). Initially, Achav was a great Torah scholar (*Sanhedrin* 103b), but then he became extremely wicked under the influence of his wife, Izevel (*Melachim* I 21:25). Eliyahu HaNavi brought Achav to repentance and publicly refuted and then killed the priests of the idol Baal at Mount Carmel.

In Yehudah:

Yehoram ruled eight years. At first, he was a tzaddik (*Horayos* 11b), but then he was influenced by his wicked wife.

Achazyahu, Yehoram's son, ruled next for two years, with wickedness.

His wicked mother, Asalyah, took over and ruled for seven years.

In 3061, the *kohein gadol*, Yehoyada, brought Yo'ash, who had been hidden as a child above the Holy of Holies in the Beis HaMikdash, to serve as king. Yo'ash became king at age seven. He ruled for forty years, but he began worshiping idols toward the end (*Divrei HaYamim* II 24:1, 24:18). He had his people kill Zecharyah, who was the *kohein gadol* and a prophet. Zecharyah's blood kept bubbling for 252 years, until the destruction of the first Beis HaMikdash.

In Yisrael:

Achazyah ben Achav ruled for two years with wickedness until he was punished.

Yehoram ben Achav ruled for twelve years.

In 3055, Yeihu began his twenty-eight-year rule (*Melachim* II 10:36). He was a great tzaddik (*Sanhedrin* 102a).

> *One-minute history lesson:* We say in Shema, "Beware...if you turn away from Hashem...there shall be no rain and the earth will fail to produce"

(*Devarim* 11:16). In the days of Achav, a three-year famine began as a result of the people's sins. This was part of the decline that eventually led to the exile of the Ten Tribes.

There are periods in history when Hashem seems to be ignoring people's choices. In truth, however, Hashem is always observing everything we do. Sooner or later everyone gets his just reward and/or punishment.

Chapter 21

Exile of the Ten Tribes

B eginning from 3100, Amatzyah, son of Yo'ash, ruled Yehudah for twenty-nine years (*Melachim* II 14:2).

Beginning from 3115, Uziyahu (Azaryah), son of Amatzyah, ruled for fifty-two years (*Melachim* II 15:2). In the twenty-seventh year of his reign, Uziyahu tried to serve as *kohein gadol* and was punished with leprosy, which lasted until the end of his life.

There were four prophets in this time period: Hoshea, Yeshayah, Amos, and Michah, with Hoshea being the greatest, or the oldest, of the group (*Pesachim* 87a).

Yeshayah began his prophecy in the twenty-seventh year of the reign of King Uziyah, the year that he was struck with leprosy (*Rashi, Yeshayah* 6:1 and 7:8).

Yeshayah lived for 120 years, 86 of which he was a prophet. The Midrash (*Devarim Rabbah* 2:4) states that he was one of the greatest of the prophets. His writings are mostly of consolation (*Bava Basra* 14b). His *sefer* is longer than that of any other prophet, and more *haftaros* come from this *sefer* than from any other, about eighteen of fifty-four.

Why did Yeshayah merit to be the prophet of consolation? The Midrash teaches it is because he always accepted the yoke of heaven with great joy (*Tanna D'vei Eliyahu Rabbah* 16).

Beginning from 3167, Yosam, son of Uziyahu, ruled for sixteen years (*Melachim* II 15:33). He was a great tzaddik, exceptional in the fulfillment of the mitzvah of honoring one's father. Rabbi Shimon bar Yochai praised him greatly (*Sukkah* 45b).

Beginning from 3183, the wicked Achaz, son of Yosam, ruled for sixteen years (ibid. 16:2). Achaz was so wicked that he would have lost everything if he hadn't demonstrated that he was ashamed of himself (*Sanhedrin* 104a).

In the kingdom of Yisrael (the Ten Tribes), Yarovam, son of Yo'ash, ruled for forty-one years (ibid. 14:23), beginning from 3113, in wickedness. Nevertheless, Hashem helped him win battles because he treated the prophets with respect (*Tanna D'vei Eliyahu Zuta* 7). This is also why he merited to be listed with the kings of Yehudah (*Pesachim* 87b). He also refused to accept an evil report against the prophet Amos.

After the death of Yarovam, Zecharyah ruled for six months in wickedness, followed by Shalom, who ruled for just one month.

The kings of Yisrael deteriorated even more after this point. Menachem ruled in Shomron in wickedness for ten years. Pekachyah ruled for two years in wickedness. Beginning from 3166, Pekach ruled for twenty years (*Melachim* II 15:27) in wickedness.

In 3187, Tiglas Pileser, king of Assyria, took the tribes of Naftali and Dan into exile (*Melachim* II 15:29).

In 3187, Hoshea took over the kingdom and ruled for eighteen years. He canceled the guards that Yarovam ben Nevat had set up to block the Jews of the Ten Tribes from coming to Yerushalayim for the festivals. This cancellation took place on the fifteenth of Av, which is one of the reasons that this is a day of joy (*Taanis* 30b). However, Hoshea was criticized for not insisting that people now go up to Yerushalayim (*Yerushalmi Taanis* 4:7).

In 3195, Shalmaneser, king of Assyria, exiled Gad, Reuven, and half of Menashe (*Rashi, Melachim* II 17:1).

In 3205, the exile of the Ten Tribes was completed. The tribes that still remained were brought to Assyria (*Melachim* II 17:23).

One-minute history lesson: The Torah (*Vayikra* 26:33 and 26:38) tells about these future exiles and why they will occur: "Because they did not listen to Hashem, and they transgressed His Covenant" (*Melachim* II 18:12).

Why did Hashem choose this form of punishment? Exile serves to humble us and to help us improve our service of Hashem.

Just as the exile of *Bnei Yisrael* was to humble the nation, "exile" of an individual serves the same purpose. When things do not seem to go well for a person — perhaps he is losing friends or financial difficulties are arising — it is a time to humble himself and improve his service of Hashem.

Chapter 22

Chizkiyahu's Reign

In 3199, Chizkiyahu, son of Achaz, became king. He ruled for twenty-nine years. During the fourteenth year of his reign, he became ill and was informed by the Prophet Yeshayah that he was going to die as a punishment for not getting married. He repented and prayed for life and thus was cured. He married the prophet's daughter and reigned for fifteen years more (*Berachos* 10a).

Chizkiyahu was unique among all the kings of Yehudah (*Melachim* II 18:5). His name signifies that Hashem strengthened him and that he strengthened the Jewish nation to serve Hashem (*Sanhedrin* 94a). The Gemara (ibid.) relates that he caused the entire nation to study Torah. Every single man, woman, boy, and girl in his time knew even the most complex halachos (*Sanhedrin* 94b).

Together with his assistants, he recorded the books of *Yeshayah*, *Mishlei*, *Shir HaShirim*, and *Koheles* (*Bava Basra* 15a).

The Midrash relates that four people in history developed their own awareness of Hashem to a unique degree: Avraham Avinu, Iyov, Chizkiyahu, and Melech HaMashiach (*Bemidbar Rabbah* 14:2).

Chizkiyahu could have been Mashiach, but he failed because he did not sing sufficient praise to Hashem (*Sanhedrin* 94a).

One-minute history lesson: When Chizkiyahu was told that he was fatally ill, he asked Yeshayah for his daughter's hand in marriage so that he could be saved. Yeshayah told Chizkiyahu that it was too late. Chizkiyahu protested that he had a tradition from David HaMelech: "Even if a sharp sword rests upon one's neck, he should not refrain from praying for mercy" (*Berachos* 10a). Thus, even in an apparently hopeless situation, a person should not give up. On the contrary, he must repent and pray for mercy.

Chizkiyahu's decision to marry and have children saved his life. His wife, Cheftzivah, literally helped save his life by marrying him. This can serve as a model for every marriage — each spouse should appreciate and value the other and realize that he or she is helping the other to succeed in this world and in the world to come.

Chapter 23

Menashe, Amon, and Yoshiyahu

In 3228, Menashe, son of Chizkiyahu, became king. He ruled for fifty-five years. He explained *sefer Vayikra* in fifty-five ways, each year of his reign with a new approach (*Sanhedrin* 103b). Although in the beginning Menashe was terribly wicked, far worse than any of his ancestors, and led *bnei Yisrael* to worship idols, he humbled himself before Hashem after being afflicted and repented thirty-three years before his death (*Seder Olam Rabbah* 24b). As a result, he lived longer and ruled more than any other king (*Divrei HaYamim* II 33:12). Rabbi Ashi once called Menashe "our colleague." That night Menashe rebuked him in a dream, and thereafter he called him "our teacher" (*Sanhedrin* 102b).

Menashe's son, Amon, was a wicked king who

ruled only two years before he was assassinated. In 3285, Amon's son Yoshiyahu became king at the age of eight. He was named by Hashem before his birth, just like Yitzchak and Shlomo (*Yerushalmi, Berachos* 1:6).

He ruled for thirty-one years (*Melachim* II 22:1). He was very righteous and was considered the greatest *baal teshuvah* in his generation (*Shabbos* 56b). At this time, a *sefer Torah* (Torah scroll) that had been concealed in the attic of the Beis HaMikdash was discovered, rolled open to the verse, "Cursed are those who fail to uphold this Torah" (*Devarim* 27:26). This caused a wave of inspiration and repentance. Not only did Yoshiyahu repent, but he also led the entire nation to repentance.

In 3302, Yirmiyahu the prophet went to Assyria and brought back exiled families from each of the Ten Tribes so that Yoshiyahu could rule over them and the entire Jewish nation could be reunited (*Megillah* 14b).

Yoshiyahu concealed the Ark before the Babylonian Exile (*Yoma* 52b).

He was killed in battle at age thirty-nine and was eulogized as if the sun had set at noontime (*Moed Katan* 25b). As he died, he said, "Hashem is righteous, and I disobeyed His instructions" (*Taanis* 22b). Although Yoshiyahu was extremely great, his downfall came about because he failed to consult the prophet Yirmiyahu before going to battle (*Taanis* 22b).

> *One-minute history lesson:* We learn from Menashe and Yoshiyahu that people in leadership positions can influence others to repent in a great way. By changing ourselves, we inspire others to follow suit. The Talmud (*Shabbos* 54b) states: "One who is able to guide his family members but fails to do so is blamed for their faults; one who can speak up to teach his city will be held responsible for them; and one who can influence the world [*Rashi* — such as a king or president] is responsible to do so."

Chapter 24

Yirmiyahu the Prophet

In the thirteenth year of the reign of Yoshiyahu, Yirmiyah began his prophecy (*Yirmiyah* 1:1). As discussed above, Yirmiyah brought back some of the Ten Tribes and Yoshiyahu ruled over them (*Megillah* 14b).

Yirmiyah is called the prophet of the destruction (*Bava Basra* 14b). He foretold the disasters that would occur if the people failed to repent sincerely and speedily. He was a *kohein* and a great tzaddik whose prayers were very potent. He was a devoted disciple of the teachings of Eliyahu the Prophet (*Targum Yonasan, Yirmiyah* 8:22).

Yirmiyah wrote the books *Yirmiyah, Melachim,* and *Eichah* (ibid. 15a). He is compared to Moshe Rabbeinu in that they both prophesied for forty years (*Pesikta D'Rav Kahana* 13:37). He was chosen for his mission even before he was born (*Yirmiyah* 1:5).

Our Sages relate that while Yirmiyah delivered

his prophecies to the people in marketplaces, the Prophet Tzefanyah spoke to the people in the synagogues and the Prophetess Chuldah spoke to the women (*Pesikta Rabbasi* 27:2).

When Yirmiyah taught that people should study more Torah, the nation replied that their time was limited because they had to earn their living. He took out the jar of *mann* that had been preserved since the time of Moshe and Aharon and explained that if they learned more Torah, Hashem would sustain them as He had sustained the Jews in the desert (*Rashi, Shemos* 4:5).

> *One-minute history lesson:* Yirmiyahu guided us through one of our most difficult periods, the destruction of the first Beis HaMikdash. We have to keep in mind that despite all the hardships we have endured Hashem promises us, "I, Hashem, have not changed, and you, the sons of Yaakov, have not perished" (*Malachi* 3:6). The Talmud teaches, "None of our tribes will ever disappear" (*Bava Basra* 115b).

Chapter 25

The Last Years of the Kingdom of Yehudah

I n 3316, Yehoyakim became king and he ruled for eleven years (*Melachim* II 23:36). Although he was a wicked king, Hashem did not destroy his generation because the people of his generation were generally righteous (*Sanhedrin* 103a). In 3320, in the fourth year of his reign, Nevuchadnetzar, King of Babylonia, came and took some of the vessels of the Beis HaMikdash and some Jews of the royal family to Babylonia (*Daniel* 1:1–2). This was the first stage of Yehudah's exile.

In 3327, Nevuchadnetzar returned to complete the second stage of the exile. He took ten thousand people, including many sages, to Babylonia. Yechezkel the Prophet was also exiled, along with King Yechanyah.

In 3327, Tzidkiyahu, son of Yoshiyahu, became

king at age 21. He ruled for eleven years (*Melachim* II 24:18), until the destruction of the First Beis HaMikdash in 3338, 410 years after it was built (*Yoma* 9b).

Tzidkiyahu is called a righteous person (*Shabbos* 149b), distinguished in his piety (*Moed Katan* 16b), perfect in his deeds (*Horayos* 11b), who atoned for his generation (*Sanhedrin* 103a). He was called *Tzidkiyahu* because he accepted Hashem's justice in destroying the Beis HaMikdash and *Shalom* because the reign of David's House came to an end in his days (*Yerushalmi, Shekalim* 6:1).

On the tenth of Teves, in the ninth year of the reign of Tzidkiyahu, the siege against Yerushalayim began (*Yirmiyah* 39:1). This is why we fast on that day. Nineteen months later, Nevuchadnetzar and his army broke into the city.

The Prophet Yirmiyah asks, "Why was the land destroyed?" (*Yirmiyah* 9:11).

This was a difficult question for the Sages and prophets to answer. The Talmud states that the First Temple was destroyed because the people failed to live up to the standard that was expected of them in avoiding the three cardinal sins: idolatry, immorality, and murder (*Yoma* 9b). However, we find in *sefer Yirmiyah* that the First Temple was destroyed "because they forsook My Torah that I set before them and because they did not hearken to follow My voice" (*Yirmiyah* 9:12). This means that although they studied Torah constantly they did not value the Torah sufficiently, and therefore they did not recite the blessings with full concentration before they learned (*Ran, Nedarim* 81a).

Whatever was the actual reason for the destruction, we need to keep in mind the teaching of our Sages (*Yoma* 9b): Because the exile in Babylonia lasted only seventy years, we learn the greatness of the Jews of that era, who were quickly able to repent and be worthy of redemption. The Second Temple, in contrast, was destroyed because of the sin of senseless hatred (ibid.). Two thousand years later, we are still waiting for the Redemption from the destruction of the Second Temple because the sin of senseless hatred still needs rectification.

One-minute history lesson: We learn from this the great resilience of the human spirit: we are capable as individuals and as a nation to persist and refuse to give up. "A tzaddik falls seven times, but he keeps on rising" (*Mishlei* 24:16). We can always pick ourselves up again to achieve great success.

Chapter 26

Exile to Babylonia

*Despite everything, even when they shall be in
the land of their enemies, I shall not reject them.*
(*Vayikra* 26:44)

In 3327, eleven years before the bulk of Jewry was
exiled to Babylonia, Nevuchadnetzar took one
thousand Jewish scholars to exile with King
Yechanyah (*Melachim* II 24:14). Mordechai joined
this group (*Esther* 2:6). Yechezkel the Prophet, a son
of Yirmiyah (*Targum Yonasan, Yechezkel* 1:3), was
also with them.

Yechezkel had begun to prophesy in Eretz Yisrael,
but his main activity was in Babylonia. His *sefer* begins with destruction and concludes with consolation (*Bava Basra* 14b). Hashem showed him the glory
of the *Shechinah* departing from the Beis HaMikdash
(*Seder Olam Rabbah* 26). When Nevuchadnetzar
called Chananyah, Mishael, and Azaryah to bow
down to an image, they consulted with Yechezkel
about the proper course of action. At that time,

Yechezkel was sent by Hashem to resurrect the dead bones (*Sanhedrin* 92b). This served to demonstrate that Hashem is the only living God, and He is in total control of life and death.

The one thousand sages were able to establish an intensive Torah community of the highest quality in Babylonia before the rest of the nation arrived. Many years earlier, Yaakov Avinu made similar preparations. After Yosef revealed himself to his brothers, he sent them to bring their father, Yaakov, and the rest of the family to Egypt in order to survive the famine. However, before Yaakov came to Egypt, he sent Yehudah ahead to establish a yeshivah in Goshen.

Some of the Sages who arrived in Babylonia before the rest of the nation were appointed to high offices, such as Daniel (*Daniel* 1:1–6). The Jewish community in Babylonia remained strong for about one thousand years.

The Gemara (*Pesachim* 87b) teaches that Hashem chose Babylonia as the place of exile for many reasons, including:

- The language of Babylonia was Aramaic, which is similar to Hebrew, thus making it easier for the exiles to cope with their new circumstances.

- Avraham Avinu was originally from this

area. Thus, the exiles would find it easier to maintain their identity.

- There was an abundance of fruit trees and linen. Thus, the exiles could establish themselves financially and have time for Torah study.

One-minute history lesson: Hashem's kindness is evident throughout history. He maneuvers and prepares our places of exile in such a way that they will be beneficial for us in many ways. We see this clearly from the *Talmud Bavli* (the Babylonian Talmud), which was developed in Babylonia. We study the *Talmud Bavli* to this day, nearly 1,500 years later, as the main source of the oral law. The *Talmud Bavli* resulted from Hashem's preparation of Babylonia as the home for the exiled Jews.

Chapter 27

The Fast of Gedalyah

In 3338, following the destruction of the first Beis HaMikdash, Nevuchadnetzar appointed a righteous leader, Gedalyah, over the remaining Jews in Eretz Yisrael. Gedalyah instructed the people to make the best of the situation, to live peacefully, and to be loyal to the king of Babylonia (*Melachim* II 25:24).

Unfortunately, Gedalyah was soon killed. He was warned that people were out to kill him, but he chose not to believe these warnings in a misguided stringency of not accepting *lashon hara* (evil talk). The halachah actually is that one should take precautions if he receives such a warning (*Niddah* 61a). We commemorate his death with the Fast of Gedalyah, the day after Rosh HaShanah. This fast is one of the fast days observed for the destruction of the Sanctuary (*Zecharyah* 8:19).

One-minute history lesson: We fast on the ninth of Av to commemorate the destruction of both Temples and on the third of Tishrei to commemorate the death of Gedalyah. From these fasts we learn that the death of the righteous is equal to the destruction of the Beis HaMikdash. Both the Temple and the righteous teach us to be aware of and to serve Hashem.

Chapter 28

Purim Turnaround

In 3390, King Koresh (Cyrus) of Persia began to rule Babylonia. He allowed the Jews to return to Yerushalayim with Zerubavel, seventy years after the first exile began in 3320. However, there was an eighteen-year delay before the rebuilding of the Second Temple began.

In 3393, King Achashveirosh, also of Persia, began his rule of fourteen years. In his third year, he celebrated the great banquet depicted at the beginning of *Megillas Esther*.

In his seventh year, he married Esther. Esther was one of the seven prophetesses in history. They are Sarah and Miriam from the Chumash, and Devorah, Chanah, Avigayil, Chuldah, and Esther of Nach (*Megillah* 14a).

According to some, Esther was one of the four most beautiful women in history: Sarah, Rachav, Avigayil, and Esther (ibid., 13a). Their outer beauty was a sign of their spiritual greatness. Esther was very modest. She would not look at any man except her husband, Mordechai (*Targum Yonasan, Esther* 2:7).

Mordechai, one of the leaders of the Jews at that time, is compared to Moshe Rabbeinu in his Torah teaching, his humility, and his assistance to the people. He was one of the great judges of the Sanhedrin, who knew seventy languages (*Esther Rabbah* 6:2).

In the twelfth year of Achashveirosh's reign, Haman issued his decree against the Jews on the thirteenth day of Nissan. The Jews fasted for three days at Esther's behest, to atone for the eating and drinking at the king's banquet (*Midrash Shochar Tov* 22:5). We are taught that the Jews "accepted the Torah anew in the days of Achashveirosh" (*Shabbos* 88a). On the sixteenth day of Nissan, Haman was hanged on the gallows he had prepared for Mordechai.

The following year, Esther, in consultation with the sages of the generation, designated the fourteenth and fifteenth days of Adar as Purim and Shushan Purim.

Achashveirosh died in the fourteenth year of his reign. His son Daryaveish (Darius of Persia) allowed the Jews to begin rebuilding the Beis HaMikdash that some year, 3407.

One-minute history lesson: The Purim miracle teaches us that Hashem always creates the remedy before He smites us (*Megillah* 13b). Esther was made queen years before the decree was enacted so that she would be able to plead on behalf of the Jews. Hashem's system is such because His whole purpose in smiting us is to alert us to improve.

Chapter 29

Ezra the Sofer

The construction of the Second Beis HaMikdash lasted four years, from 3408 to 3412. Although it was physically similar to the First Temple, it lacked five significant things: 1) the Heavenly fire, 2) the Aron (Ark), 3) the *urim vetumim* (precious stones through which the *kohein gadol* sought advice from Hashem), 4) anointing oil, and 5) the spirit of prophecy (*Yoma* 21b).

In 3413, Ezra HaSofer (Ezra the Sage) came up to Eretz Yisrael from Babylonia. Ezra was a *kohein*. He had received authorization from King Artachshasta to form the Great Assembly of Jewish leaders, the Anshei Knessess HaGedolah (see *Ezra* 7:25).

Ezra could have brought us the Torah from Mount Sinai had Moshe Rabbeinu not preceded him (*Sanhedrin* 21b). The Midrash teaches that he could have done the job of Aharon HaKohen (*Koheles Rabbah* 1:4). As long as his rebbe, Baruch, was alive, Ezra would not leave Babylonia to go to Eretz Yisrael

(*Megillah* 16b). This is the way of all great Torah Sages, as we see from Yehoshua, who served his rebbe, Moshe (*Shemos* 33:11), and Elisha, who served Eliyahu HaNavi (*Melachim* II 3:11). This is why Hashem chose him to become the greatest teacher from his time onward (Rav Avigdor Miller, *Torah Nation*, p. 51).

At this time, the Jews could have had great miracles occur for them, as in the days of Yehoshua bin Nun when the whole nation came to Eretz Yisrael the first time, but they were not meritorious enough.
(*Berachos* 4a)

When the Torah was weak in Eretz Yisrael, Ezra came from Babylonia and fortified it.
(*Sukkah* 20a)

Ezra and his *beis din* instituted ten *takanos* (rules): two to increase Torah study, one to have judges available, one to help people prepare for Shabbos, one to help the poor, three to help women with *tzenius* (modesty) and to enhance their beauty, one to help men with *mikveh*, and one to help increase the Jewish nation (*Bava Kama* 82a). Thus we see that they focused on all aspects of the needs of our nation.

One-minute history lesson: Hashem places

unique, gifted people at critical times in history to inspire and transform the world. "Ezra prepared himself to learn and teach Hashem's Torah" (*Ezra* 7:10).

Chapter 30

The Sages of the Great Assembly

he Great Assembly was composed of 120 Sages, including eighty prophets. These Sages were the bridge between the age of prophecy and the era of the *tannaim* (the Sages who taught the Mishnah), as it says at the beginning of *Pirkei Avos*: "Moshe received the Torah from Sinai and transmitted it to Yehoshua; Yehoshua to the Elders; the Elders to the Prophets; and the Prophets transmitted it to the Sages of the Great Assembly..." (*Avos* 1:1).

The Sages of the Great Assembly lived by and taught three rules:

Be patient in judgment, teach many disciples, and make a fence for the Torah.
(Ibid.)

They instituted the main decrees of the Sages, formulated the texts of our prayers, and arranged and completed the Books of *Yechezkel*, the Twelve Minor Prophets, *Daniel*, and *Esther* (*Bava Basra* 14b).

The Sages of the Great Assembly sealed the Scriptures, with the guarantee that every word included in Tanach (the Torah, Prophets, and Writings) is full of profound and unlimited wisdom and secrets. Every statement is the absolute truth of Hashem's Torah (Rav Avigdor Miller, *Torah Nation*, p. 67).

One-minute history lesson: The Sages of the Great Assembly assured us that Jewish history has no gaps when they sealed the Scriptures. The Torah begins with *Bereishis*, the creation of the world; continues through Tanach with the major and minor prophets; and concludes with the Sages of the Great Assembly. The Rambam further outlines the Torah's transmission to the Sages of the Mishnah and Gemara. Following him are the *rishonim* and *acharonim* until today, who continue to transmit the Torah to each succeeding generation.

Part 4

Age of the Tannaim

Chapter 31

Shimon HaTzaddik

The *tannaim* are the Sages whose teachings of the oral tradition were eventually preserved in written form in the Mishnah.

In 3448, the era of the *tannaim* began with Shimon HaTzaddik (Shimon the Righteous), the *kohein gadol*.

In 3448, Alexander the Great set out to conquer Yerushalayim. Shimon HaTzaddik went out to meet him and placate him. As soon as Alexander saw him, he dismounted and bowed before him. Alexander's followers were shocked that the great king was bowing before a Jew. Alexander explained himself: Before every battle, a vision of Shimon HaTzaddik appeared before him and assured him of victory. Shimon said to him, "Will you destroy the Temple in which we pray for your welfare?" As a result, he would not lay a hand against Yerushalayim (*Yoma* 69a).

Shimon was *kohein gadol* for forty years and

Hashem favored him with many miraculous blessings, such as the *lechem hapanim* (the showbread) remaining fresh from one Shabbos to the next Shabbos, as if straight from the oven. This was an exception for the Second Temple period, not the rule as it had been during the First Temple. He passed away in 3488.

> *One-minute history lesson:* Although Shimon HaTzaddik taught numerous teachings over his forty years of leadership, *Pirkei Avos* teaches us his famous motto: "The world stands on three pillars: on Torah, on service [of Hashem], and on acts of loving kindness" (*Avos* 1:2). We need to follow the practice of saying this statement always so that it becomes our way of life.

Chapter 32

The Translation

I n 3500 (some say 3515), seventy-two Torah scholars were coerced by King Ptolemy to translate the
Torah into Greek (*Megillah* 9a).

This event was considered as tragic as the sin of
the golden calf (*Sofrim* 1:7). Just as the golden calf
had been intended as a means to come close to
Hashem but instead brought great calamity to the
Jewish nation, so, too, the Egyptian Jews encouraged
Ptolemy to have the Torah translated in order to
bring it honor but instead only damaged the Torah's
honor (Rav Avigdor Miller, *Torah Nation*, para. 228).
Nevertheless, Hashem miraculously guided each of
the seventy-two Sages to make thirteen identical
changes — to avoid some misunderstandings by
gentile readers of the translations.

It pays to learn these thirteen editorial alterations, as set forth in *Megillah* 9a–b, in order to see
how we need to adjust translations for accuracy and
truth. In addition, the text gives us an appreciation

of the intricacies of this unusual miracle — thirteen identical alterations by seventy-two individual Sages who were working in isolation!

One-minute history lesson: When we learn something from a translation of the original, we gain and lose at the same time. For example, if we read a Torah verse in English it may be easier to understand, but we miss much of the flavor of Hashem's words, which are filled with unlimited wisdom and secrets. Every word is meaningful and loaded with nuances of profound significance. We must strive to learn how to appreciate original Torah sources.

Chapter 33

Leadership Teams

In 3550, the Sanhedrin (the ruling body of the nation) instituted the new office of *nasi*. The *nasi* would be the leader of the Sages and the spokesman for the nation. The first Sage to hold this position was Yosei ben Yoezer, a *kohein*. He was known as the Pious *Kohein* (*Chagigah* 18b).

His colleague, Yosei ben Yochanan, was the *av beis din*, the head of the court system.

These two Sages composed the first pair: one head of the Sages for general matters and one head of the legal system. They taught the people how to develop Torah study and *chesed* in one's home. For example, Yosei ben Yoezer taught, "Make your home a meeting place for Sages and drink their words with thirst" (*Avos* 1:4). Yosei ben Yochanan taught, "Welcome poor people to your home and do not speak much idle talk with women" (ibid., 5).

Until the end of Yosei ben Yoezer's life they

studied Torah as by Moshe Rabbeinu — that is,
without disputes. The first dispute took place over
one of the laws concerning a korban [sacrifice]
on yom tov.
(*Temurah* 15b)

In 3610, the second pair, Yehoshua ben Perachyah and Nittai HaArbeili, became the leaders. They focused on teaching how to avoid the wrong environment and develop the right one, as we learn in *Avos*, "Yehoshua ben Perachyah says: "Accept a teacher upon yourself, and acquire for yourself a friend" (1:6), while Nittai HaArbeili said, "Keep far away from the wicked" (1:7).

In 3688, Shimon ben Shetach (as *nasi*) and Yehudah ben Tabbai (as *av beis din*) became the leaders.

Also in 3688, Shemayah and Avtalyon served as the leaders.

In 3729, Hillel and Shammai became the leaders. These Sages taught us some of the most fundamental Torah rules for success in life:

- "Love peace" (Hillel, ibid., 12).

- "Love people" (Hillel, ibid., 12).

- "Do it now" (Hillel, ibid., 14).

- "Receive all people with a kindly, thoughtful face" (Shammai, ibid., 15).

One-minute history lesson: In each era we see how the Sages focused their efforts on specific Torah ideals. Although we have to always keep in mind all of the Torah's lessons, in each generation we need to emphasize the specific areas that address the unique challenges of our time. We need to find slogans for our generation to accomplish our goals in life.

Chapter 34

The Chanukah Miracle

In 3616, the Syrian-Greeks, who ruled Eretz Yisrael at the time, began imposing decrees against Jews. They enacted laws against Shabbos, bris milah, and marriage (*Kesubos* 3b, *Sanhedrin* 32b).

Hashem has a system of *middah keneged middah*, measure for measure (see *Mishlei* 28:9; *Avos* 2:4); which means that He deals with us based upon the way we act. He performs miracles on our behalf when we extend ourselves to defend His Name (*Berachos* 20a).

Thus, in 3622, the Chashmonaim began to fight the Greeks, to defend the honor of Hashem. Matisyahu, a *kohein*, gathered his five sons and others loyal to Hashem to fight.

On the twenty-fifth of Kislev, the Chashmonaim were able to rededicate the new Mizbei'ach (altar). However, they found only one measure of pure olive oil with which to kindle the Menorah. Miraculously, this oil burned for eight days. This was a clear sign that the Chashmonaim were favored by Hashem, as in the days of Shimon HaTzaddik (see chapter 31), when the western light would always burn miraculously (*Yoma* 39a). This miracle served as a testimony that the *Shechinah*, the Divine Presence, was with us (*Shabbos* 22b).

One-minute history lesson: Our foremost goal in life should be to be close to Hashem. When we do what Hashem requires of us, Hashem favors us with His Presence — measure for measure.

Hashem is your Guardian; Hashem is your shadow at your right hand.
(*Tehillim* 121:5)

Chapter 35

The Chashmonai Kings

After the victory over the Greeks, Shimon, son of Matisyahu, became the *nasi*, leader of the nation. Upon his death in 3642, Yochanan Hyrcanus, his son, became the *nasi*. Yochanan Hyrcanus also served as *kohein gadol* for eighty years. But at the end of his life, his sympathies for the Tzedukim (a group that did not accept the Divine origin of the oral law) were exposed.

Do not trust yourself until the day of your death.
(*Avos* 2:5; *Berachos* 29a)

In *Kiddushin* (66a), we learn of a king who turned sour and killed the Jewish Sages. Rava says this episode is about Yochanan Hyrcanus.

After Yochanan Hyrcanus died, two more generations of Chashmonaim ruled the people. However, they were not loyal to the Torah and persecuted the Sages. In 3742, Hordus, a slave of the Chashmonaim, took over the throne and killed the Sages (*Bava Basra* 3b).

The Ramban (on *Bereishis* 49:10) explains why the family of the Chashmonaim died out: "Although they were at first greatly devoted to Hashem and kept the Torah and mitzvos from being forgotten [during the Chanukah era], their reign did not last. Their slaves eventually took over and destroyed them. The underlying problem was that they were not descendants of David HaMelech. Thus, they were not entitled to be rulers."

One-minute history lesson: Long-term success, on both a national and a personal level, requires adherence to all the laws of the Torah. Power corrupts when people lose sight of who is in control. Hashem is the master of all and He is the one who decides who is entitled to power.

Chapter 36

Saving the Torah

Duaring the reign of the Chashmonaim, an important change was made in the educational system in Eretz Yisrael. Queen Shlomis, wife of Alexander Yannai, was able to bring her brother, Shimon ben Shetach (a member of the third pair, along with Yehudah ben Tabbai, see chapter 33), back from exile. (The Sages had been exiled by Alexander Yannai, a wicked Chashmonai king.)

> *The world was desolate until Shimon ben Shetach restored the Torah to its place of grandeur.*
> (*Kiddushin* 66a)

Meanwhile, King Alexander Yannai appointed Yehoshua ben Gamla as *kohein gadol* (*Yevamos* 61a). "Yehoshua ben Gamla is to be remembered for good because he saved the Torah by instituting a system to provide the children of every town with schools in which to study Torah" (*Bava Basra* 21a).

Yehoshua ben Gamla and Shimon ben Shetach worked together to make this school system a reality.

The Gemara (ibid.) tells us how the education system of that time was developed: At first, every father would teach his son Torah. Then a central yeshivah was started in Yerushalayim for orphans who had no one to teach them. But since there were orphans who had no one to bring them to this central location, the Sages instituted yeshivos in every province for teenagers.

This was not always sufficient, so Yehoshua ben Gamla instituted yeshivos in every city with students starting from the age of six or seven. This program finally solved all of the educational problems.

In the days of Shimon ben Shetach prosperity
was restored.
(Taanis 23a)

When the righteous have authority, the nation
rejoices.
(Mishlei 29:2)

One-minute history lesson: After every decline (in this case, the downfall of the Chashmonai kings), Hashem provides opportunities for growth and achievement.

Chapter 37

Hillel

In 3728, Hillel and Shammai became the leaders of the nation. Hillel, who was from the family of David HaMelech, became the *nasi*, while Shammai became the leader of the *beis din*.

Hillel began as a very poor individual. He almost froze to death once in his attempt to study Torah (*Yoma* 35b). His enthusiasm and devotion to Torah eventually brought him to supreme greatness. He is an illustration of the maxim set forth in *Makkos* (10b): "On the path one is determined to go, he will be led." Hillel became *nasi* at the age of eighty and led the nation for forty years. His example of character and devotion to Torah and his many great teachings live on forever.

Hillel is listed as one of three great personalities in our history, who, each in his own era, saved the Torah from being forgotten (the other two were Ezra before him and Rabbi Chiya after him) [*Sukkah* 20a]. He is also listed with four great leaders who lived 120 years: Moshe Rabbeinu, Hillel, Rabbi Yochanan ben Zakkai, and Rabbi Akiva (*Tosafos, Bechoros* 58a).

Hillel had eighty major disciples, thirty of whom were worthy of having the Shechinah rest upon them, as by Moshe Rabbeinu; thirty of whom were worthy of stopping the sun, as by Yehoshua ben Nun [see Yehoshua 10:12]; and the remaining twenty, who were average. The eldest of them was Yonasan ben Uziel [who wrote an Aramaic translation of Tanach], and the youngest was Rabbi Yochanan ben Zakkai.
(*Sukkah* 28a)

Hillel's unique humility influenced others and drew many to come close to the *Shechinah* (*Shabbos* 31a). He taught that the entire Torah stands on the principle, "Treat others the way you would like to be treated" (*Shabbos* 31a). Shammai was also extremely humble. He is the Sage who is famous for his maxim, "Greet every person with a thoughtful, pleasant countenance" (*Avos* 1:15).

Hillel passed away in 3768, sixty years before the destruction of the Second Beis HaMikdash. Upon his death, Rabban Shimon ben Hillel became *nasi*.

Forty years before the Churban, Rabbi Tzaddok began to fast daily in an attempt to prevent the Churban (*Gittin* 56a).

One-minute history lesson: "Hillel obligates

the poor" (*Yoma* 35b). On the day of judgment, everyone will be asked if he studied Torah. Some people may reply that they were too poor to make time for Torah study. They will be challenged, "Were you poorer than Hillel?"

Chapter 38

The Destruction of the Second Temple

I n 3788, the Sanhedrin was exiled. "Forty years before the Churban [destruction], the members of the Sanhedrin left their special chambers in the Sanctuary" (*Shabbos* 15a).

In 3828 (68 C.E.), the Second Beis HaMikdash was destroyed by Titus the Wicked. It had stood for 420 years, during which Eretz Yisrael was ruled by Persia for 34 years, Greece for 180 years, the Chashmonaim for 103 years, and Hordus for 103 years (*Avodah Zarah* 9a).

The destruction was a result of *sinas chinam* (senseless hatred) amongst some Jews (*Yoma* 9b). Hashem's purpose in allowing the Second Temple to be destroyed was analogous to smashing a keg of honey in order to destroy a serpent coiled around it (*Gittin* 56b). As a result of the Temple's destruction, we became cleansed of the disloyal members of our nation and restored as a people who adhere to the Torah's laws.

Toward the end of the three-year siege around Yerushalayim, Rabbi Yochanan ben Zakkai left the city concealed in a coffin. Once outside, he arranged to meet with Vespasian, the general in charge of besieging the city. Rabbi Yochanan ben Zakkai made a good impression on Vespasian. As a result, Vespasian granted his request to spare the Sages when he destroyed the city (*Gittin* 56b), thus rescuing our nation from spiritual destruction, *chas veshalom*.

The second Holy Temple was set on fire by the Romans on the Ninth of Av, the same day as the destruction of the First Beis HaMikdash, 490 years earlier. This "coincidence" was an obvious sign that both Temples were destroyed by Hashem for similar reasons.

One-minute history lesson: We fast every year on the Ninth of Av, Tishah B'Av, in order to commemorate the events surrounding the destruction of the two Temples and all the other tragedies that have occurred throughout Jewish history. We pray constantly for the rebuilding of the Beis HaMikdash. How will the rebuilding of the Temple make everything better? Will the enemies of the Jewish people disappear with the mere building of this structure?

The rebuilding of the Temple refers to more than a physical edifice. It will be the start of a new era, a return to our "Days of Old," a time when our principal pursuit will be to know Hashem and His Torah.

May that time come speedily in our days!

Chapter 39

Rabbi Yochanan ben Zakkai

Rabbi Yochanan ben Zakkai, like his rebbe Hillel (see chapter 37), lived for 120 years. "Since the destruction of the Holy Temple, Hashem's focus is on the places where Torah is studied" (*Berachos* 8a). All the Torah that we have now was transmitted by Rabbi Yochanan's five major disciples. They preserved Hashem's Torah through their efforts at their great yeshivah in Yavneh.

Rabbi Yochanan ben Zakkai would always enumerate the praises of his five disciples (*Avos* 2:11):

1. Rabbi Eliezer ben Hyrcanus — perfect recall.

2. Rabbi Yehoshua ben Chananyah — fortunate was the one who gave birth to him.

3. Rabbi Yosei HaKohen — the pious one.

4. Rabbi Shimon ben Nesanel — afraid of sin.

5. Rabbi Elazar ben Aroch — creative mind.

The first two Sages listed, Rabbi Eliezer ben Hyrcanus and Rabbi Yehoshua ben Chananyah, were the teachers of Rabbi Akiva (see next chapter). They were also the teachers of Onkelos, a convert who became a great Sage and wrote an Aramaic translation of the Torah, which is included in most *chumashim*. We are required to read this commentary every week to understand the weekly Torah portion (see *Shulchan Aruch, Orach Chaim* 285).

Rabbi Yochanan ben Zakkai did not take credit for his vast Torah knowledge because he acknowledged that we were created for the purpose of learning (*Avos* 2:9).

He was humble toward all. He was always the first to greet everyone, whether Jew or non-Jew, even on the street (*Berachos* 17a).

One-minute history lesson: There are four great personalities in Jewish history who lived 120 years: Moshe Rabbeinu, Hillel, Rabbi Yochanan ben Zakkai, and Rabbi Akiva (*Tosafos, Bechoros* 58a). They were all similar in that they led the Jewish nation for the last forty years of their lives, and their lives were divided into three segments of forty years.

This serves as a model for us. We need to

live with ambition, realizing that the best is yet
to come. We must have faith that, as we strive
to perfect ourselves, Hashem will assist us more
and more. We should increase our efforts in
learning and teaching Torah and doing more
mitzvos as we get older.

Chapter 40

Rabbi Akiva

Rabbi Akiva did not begin learning Torah until the age of forty. His wife, Rachel, was the one who motivated him to greatness. He publicly gave her credit for his learning with famous proclamation to his students: "My Torah and your Torah are due to her" (*Nedarim* 50a). He also taught, "Who is truly wealthy? He who has a good wife" (*Shabbos* 25b).

Two of Rabbi Yochanan's students, Rabbi Eliezer ben Hyrcanus and Rabbi Yehoshua ben Chananyah, became Rabbi Akiva's teachers. Rabbi Akiva was also a student of Nachum Ish Gamzu (*Chagigah* 12a), who lived by the phrase "This, too, is for the good" (*Taanis* 21a). Rabbi Akiva lived by a similar, but more explanatory, phrase: "All that the Merciful One does is for good" (*Berachos* 60b). (For more on this topic, see our book, *The Road to Greatness* [Targum Press, 1997], Section Three, "Learning to Laugh with Rabbi Akiva.")

Rabbi Akiva lived to the age of 120. He lived for about sixty years before the destruction of the Second Temple, and about sixty years afterwards.

Even before the destruction of the Second Temple, Rabbi Akiva had 24,000 disciples (Rav Avigdor Miller, *Exalted People*, p. 74). However, they all passed away due to their failure to give sufficient honor to each other (*Yevamos* 62b).

After their death, he started a new yeshivah, where he taught the following students:

1. Rabbi Meir, to whom most anonymous *mishnayos* are attributed.

2. Rabbi Yehudah bar Ila'i, author of anonymous teachings of *Sifra*, the famous commentary on *Vayikra*.

3. Rabbi Yosei ben Chalafta, who is credited with writing *Seder Olam Rabbah*, the source of much of the historical data from Creation to his day.

4. Rabbi Shimon bar Yochai, author of the *Zohar* and *Sifri*, the commentary on *Bemidbar* and *Devarim*. (See chapter 42 below.)

5. Rabbi Elazar ben Shammua, a teacher of Rabbi Yehudah HaNasi, who redacted the Mishnah.

All that Rabbi Akiva's disciples taught was based on their rebbe's teachings (*Sanhedrin* 81a). We see that together they taught and explained the entire Torah.

To help Rabbi Akiva succeed, Hashem granted him considerable wealth six times from various sources (*Nedarim* 50b).

Rabbi Tarfon said, "Forsaking Rabbi Akiva is like forsaking one's life" (*Kiddushin* 66b).

He was exceptionally humble and yielding (*Taanis* 25b).

The Sages of the Sanhedrin went to ten places after being exiled from the Beis HaMikdash (*Rosh HaShanah* 31a). First they went to Yavneh, then to Usha, then back to Yavneh, and then back to Usha. The second time at Usha, Rabbi Akiva was *nasi* of the Sanhedrin.

One-minute history lesson: Rabbi Akiva did not begin to study Torah until he was forty years old. Everything that he accomplished started after forty years of ignorance. It is never too late to study Torah and even to become a great Torah scholar. As Rabbi Akiva himself teaches:

Permission is granted...and everything depends on the abundance of one's actions.
(*Avos* 3:15)

Chapter 41

The Fall of Beitar

*The fall of Beitar was a great tragedy, equal to
that of the destruction of the Beis HaMikdash.*
(Rambam, *Taanis* 5:3)

I n 3892 (132 C.E.), on the ninth of Av, sixty-three
years after the destruction of the Second Beis
HaMikdash, Beitar was captured by the Romans
and more than 500,000 Jews were killed.

The Gemara (*Berachos* 48b) relates that when the
Romans granted permission to the Jews to bury the
victims of Beitar fifteen years after they had been
killed, the Sages of Yavneh instituted the fourth
blessing of *Birkas HaMazon* (Grace after Meals) to
perpetuate our gratitude to Hashem for His goodness. Not only were the Jews now allowed to bury the
bodies, but the bodies had also been miraculously
preserved from decay.

In 3893, Rabbi Akiva was arrested by the
Romans, at the age of 120, for teaching Torah publicly (*Berachos* 61b). He was killed on the fifth day of

Tishrei in the midst of saying the Shema. He told his students that he had been waiting all his life for the opportunity to give his life back to Hashem. His soul left him as he was extending the word *echad* in the Shema. A Heavenly voice then proclaimed, "You are fortunate, Rabbi Akiva, that your soul departed with *echad*...and you are prepared for entry into the world to come" (ibid).

> *When Rabbi Akiva was killed, the glory of Torah*
> *was diminished.*
> (*Sotah* 49a)

The Talmud also teaches, "When Rabbi Akiva died, Rabbeinu HaKadosh [Rabbi Yehudah HaNasi, the redactor of the Mishnah] was already born." This demonstrates the principle of the "sun shines and the sun sets" (*Koheles* 1:5), i.e., as one great Torah luminary passes on, Hashem provides us with another (*Kiddushin* 72b).

One-minute history lesson: The Sages used the burial of the Jews of Beitar as an opportunity to demonstrate that Hashem is still with us in exile and that He will continue to guide and protect us to the end of time. The text that they added to *Birkas HaMazon* is a glorious review of Hashem's goodness to us throughout history, past, present, and future. It is one of the most significant themes in history: Hashem is with us and all that He does is for our own benefit!

Chapter 42

A Conversation about the Romans

Rabbi Yehudah bar Ila'i, Rabbi Yosei, and Rabbi Shimon bar Yochai were once having a discussion. Rabbi Yehudah praised the Romans for rebuilding the cities and roads, Rabbi Yosei was silent, and Rabbi Shimon criticized the Romans, saying they had built the cities and roads for ulterior motives (*Shabbos* 33b).

As a result, the Romans elevated Rabbi Yehudah to become the leading spokesman at all Jewish assemblies. Rabbi Yosei was exiled to Tzippori, while Rabbi Shimon was sentenced to death. This generation was known as the generation of Rabbi Yehudah bar Ila'i (*Sanhedrin* 20a). The Talmud (*Nedarim* 49b) describes a series of incidents which demonstrate that Rabbi Yehudah always focused on the positive in everything.

Rabbi Yosei is famous for being a very insightful sage and a deep thinker (*Gittin* 67a). He is the author of *Seder Olam*, a compilation of the chronological patterns of Jewish history (*Yevamos* 82b).

Rabbi Shimon and his son, Elazar, hid from the Romans in a cave for thirteen and a half years. During this time, they immersed themselves in Torah and subsisted on carobs. Both improved their scholarship greatly. Rabbi Shimon is especially famous for writing the *Zohar* (teachings on Kabbalah, Jewish mysticism). He passed away on the thirty-third day of the Omer (Lag BaOmer) and is buried in Meron, near Tzefas.

One-minute history lesson: The miraculous manner in which Rabbi Shimon bar Yochai and his son Elazar survived following their flight from the Romans illustrates how Hashem has ways of testing people in different situations and helping them to achieve greatness so that they can later serve the Jewish nation.

In addition, the way in which Hashem promoted Rabbi Yehudah to a position of influence is also noteworthy. It enabled him to lead the generation at that time and for always afterwards. His positive teachings are all over *Shas* and are studied and practiced by Jews everywhere.

Chapter 43

The Writing of the Mishnah

At the close of the period of the *tannaim*, Rabbi Yehudah HaNasi became the leading sage of his generation. He is called Rabbeinu HaKadosh, our holy teacher, because of his unique holiness (*Shabbos* 18b). The term "Rebbe" by itself always refers to Rabbi Yehudah HaNasi.

From the days of Moshe Rabbeinu until Rebbe,
we do not find such a great person with Torah
and power united.
(*Gittin* 59a)

Hashem arranged that Rebbe and the Roman Emperor, Marcus Aurelius, should meet (*Avodah Zarah* 10b). They became friends, and the Emperor backed and supported Rebbe, enabling him to devote his time and efforts to completing and sealing the Mishnah for all time. This friendship was one of the great miracles Hashem performed for His people in order to facilitate the closing of the Mishnah (Rav Avigdor Miller, *Exalted People*, p. 167).

The work of writing the oral Torah was begun by Rabbi Nassan, who came to Eretz Yisrael from Babylonia in 3904 (144 C.E.). Rabbi Nassan was so great that he was appointed *av beis din*. He began the task of editing the Mishnah — the teachings of Hashem from Sinai — which Rabbi Yehudah HaNasi completed (*Bava Metzia* 86a).

Rebbe began organizing the Mishnah in approximately 3924 (164 C.E.) and finished it in 3948 (188 C.E.). "Rebbe and Rabbi Nassan sealed the Mishnah" (*Bava Metzia* 86a). The Mishnah was completed 120 years after the destruction of the Second Temple, 1,500 years after the Torah was received at Sinai and 500 years after the last prophet in 3448.

One-minute history lesson: The Mishnah and its commentary, the Gemara, are the works that enable the Jewish people to follow the teachings of the Torah and uphold its covenant with Hashem forever (*Gittin* 60b). When the Sages saw the opportunity to finalize and seal the Mishnah, they utilized it to ensure the continuity of the holy Torah. We learn from this that when opportunities such as a new *shiur* in our community or an offer to learn with a good *chavrusa* come our way, we should consider applying the principle, "If not now, when?" (*Avos* 1:14).

Chapter 44

The End of the Period of the Tannaim

After nearly two thousand years of tremendous Torah growth, from the teachings of Avraham to the sealing of the Mishnah, this era was coming to a close (see chapter 7).

At this time, "when the Torah was being forgotten, Rabbi Chiya and his sons, came to reestablish it" (*Sukkah* 20a). Rabbi Chiya thus joined two of his predecessors who performed similar feats in their time: Ezra reestablished the Torah in his time (see chapter 29), and Hillel did the same in his time (see chapter 37).

> *How great are the deeds of Rabbi Chiya in teaching Torah all over!*
> (*Bava Metzia* 85b)

The Gemara (ibid.) relates that Reish Lakish, a

later Sage, heard a *bas kol* (heavenly voice) that said, "You have accomplished like Rabbi Chiya in *pilpul* [analytical analysis], but you did not spread Torah as he did...."

Rabbi Chiya would plant flax to prepare nets for trapping deer. He fed the deer meat to orphans and used their hides to prepare *sefarim* with which he taught. He would travel from town to town and teach groups of five children, each one a different *Chumash*, with the instructions that they each teach the others in their group their *Chumash*. Thus, he devised a system that spread Torah throughout the Jewish nation.

As noted earlier, Rabbi Yehudah HaNasi arranged the Mishnah in its final form. There were, however, teachings that Rebbe did not explain in the Mishnah. Rabbi Chiya and Rabbi Oshaya gathered these teachings into a collection referred to as *Beraisos*. Every statement in the *Beraisos* of Rabbi Chiya and Rabbi Oshaya had its source in a *mishnah* (*Kesubos* 69b). The *Beraisos* were thus commentaries on the Mishnah (*Eiruvin* 92a). These *Beraisos* are found throughout the Gemara and are, generally, introduced by such phrases as "our Rabbis taught" or "it has been taught."

One-minute history lesson: Even after it seems that everything has already been done, there are improvements that can be made. The *mishnayos* were all sealed and yet Rabbi Chiya came along with explanations and methods of outreach that helped change the world.

History is still in the making and each of us is required to utilize our potential to help ourselves and others grow great, as the Talmud teaches, "My predecessors left me a place to become renowned" (*Chullin 7a*).

Part 5

Age of the Amoraim

Chapter 45

First of the Amoraim

Rav, Shmuel, and Rabbi Yochanan were three great Sages who laid the foundation of all the discussions of the *amoraim* in the Gemara. The Gemara (*Avodah Zarah* 40a) says that they were called "*karoi*," because their words are as solid as a verse in Scripture (*Rashi*).

Rav's name was Abba, but he was called "Rav" to signify his unique greatness (*Rashbam, Bava Basra* 52a). He was Rabbi Chiya's nephew, and he came to Eretz Yisrael from Babylonia with his uncle. Forty-four years later, in 3979 (219 C.E.) he returned to the Babylonian city Sura and became the leading Sage there until his death at the age of ninety. Rav was born toward the end of the period of the *tannaim* and, although he was considered an *amora* (a Sage of the Gemara), he had traditions that he had learned from the last of the *tannaim*. Thus, he had the status of a *tanna* in some cases.

Rav was a disciple of Rebbe (*Gittin* 69a).

He composed some of our prayers. His personal prayer, which he said at the conclusion of the Shemoneh Esrei, was to merit long life (*Berachos* 16b).

His home in Babylonia was called a miniature Beis HaMikdash (*Megillah* 29a) because he was so wise, holy, and righteous.

When people would honor him, he would recite verses from Tanach to remind himself to be humble (*Sanhedrin* 7b).

He never walked a distance greater than four *amos* (about eight feet) without Torah study, tzitzis, and tefillin (*Rambam, Hilchos Tefillin* 4:25).

He never spoke idle talk (*Rambam, Hilchos Dei'os* 2:4).

He wrote *sefarim* to explain the Mishnah (*Hakdamas HaRambam*).

We follow his opinion in matters of forbidden things because he was extensively involved in decisions on those issues (*Rosh, Bava Kama* 4:4).

*   *   *

Rav's Torah partner was Shmuel, who became the Torah leader in Babylonia after Rav's passing. Often the Gemara mentions two opposite points of view: one of Rav and one of Shmuel.

Shmuel was a *kohein*. He was also known as an expert in medicine and astronomy. He said that he knew the pathways of the skies as well as he knew the streets of the Babylonian city Neharda'a (*Berachos* 58b).

We follow Shmuel's view in monetary issues because that was his specialty (*Berachos* 49b). Some of his famous teachings are:

- "The law of the government is law" (*Gittin* 58b).

- "We do not follow the majority in monetary issues" (*Bava Kama* 46b).

- "One who has a claim against others needs to provide proof" (ibid.).

Rav said about him, "All secrets are revealed to you" (*Chullin* 59b).

Shmuel did not have official *semichah* (Rabbinical ordination). Rebbe attempted to give him *semichah* due to his greatness, but it did not materialize. Shmuel then said, "I saw the *sefer* of Adam HaRishon which recorded all future leaders in history. There it said that Shmuel would be a great Sage, but he would not receive the title of *semichah*" (*Bava Metzia* 85b).

*   *   *

Rabbi Yochanan, the leader in Eretz Yisrael beginning from 4014, was an orphan of both parents from birth. He inherited great wealth, which he used to support himself and to study Torah.

He inspired Reish Lakish to repent and change his evil ways. Reish Lakish became a great Torah scholar who would ask twenty-four questions of Rabbi Yochanan on each topic discussed between them (*Bava Metzia* 84a).

Rabbi Yochanan is the main teacher of *Talmud Yerushalmi*.

He spent three days memorizing *Sifra* and then three months analyzing what he had memorized (*Yevamos* 72b).

We follow his rulings, even when they are against those of Rav and Shmuel.

One-minute history lesson: Rav and Shmuel were colleagues who loved and respected each other. In most issues, they agreed; however, when they disagreed, they debated to clarify the issues. When Rav passed away, Shmuel tore thirteen of his garments and said, "The man I feared has departed" (*Moed Katan* 24a). It is important to remember that when true Torah scholars disagree they never extend their disagreement to a personal level.

Chapter 46

Second Generation of Amoraim

Rav Huna, the chief disciple of Rav, became the leading Sage of Babylonia in 4016 (256 C.E.). He led for forty years. (There are actually four Rav Hunas in the Gemara, one earlier than this one and two later.)

Rav Huna was the head of the Sura Yeshivah in Babylonia. When Rava, a later Sage (see chapter 48), would pray for greatness, he would ask for three attributes: "wisdom like Rav Huna, wealth like Rav Chisda, and humility like Rabbah ben Rav Huna" (*Moed Katan* 28a).

Rav Huna's involvement in spreading Torah is compared to the unique deeds of Rabbi Chiya (see chapter 44) [*Moed Katan* 25a].

In the *Talmud Yerushalmi* (*Chagigah* 1:8), Rav Huna is called "leader of leaders." Of him it was said: "He was worthy that the *Shechinah* should rest on him, had he not lived in Babylonia" (*Moed Katan* 25a).

*   *   *

Rabbi Yehudah (not to be confused with Rabbi Yehudah HaNasi, see chapter 43) was the leading Sage in 4058 (298 C.E.). He studied first under Rav, until his passing, and then under Shmuel (see Chapter 45) [*Rashbam, Bava Basra* 38b].

*   *   *

Rav Chisda was also a leading Sage about this time (4060/300 C.E.).

He was very great in *pilpul*, a sharp, deeply analytical method of studying the Gemara (*Eiruvin* 67b).

One of his specialities was teaching Torah topics regarding health matters, saving money, and marital success (*Shabbos* 140b). He also taught the need to make *simanim* (mnemonic devices used as aids to memorizing various subjects) to acquire Torah (*Eiruvin* 54b).

Rav Chisda was called the "chassid" (pious one) of Babylonia (*Taanis* 23b). The Angel of Death found it difficult to approach him because of his nonstop Torah study (*Moed Katan* 28a).

He lived to the age of ninety-two, and he had six sons and three sons-in-law. His sons-in-law were all exceptional scholars: Rava (see chapter 48), Romi bar Chama, and Mar Ukva bar Chama.

One-minute history lesson: Do we pray for wisdom? Do we pray for humility? Like Rava, we should strive to achieve the levels of those who came before us. The Gemara (*Berachos* 50a) teaches one to "open his mouth wide in Torah matters," i.e., one should pray for great goals when it comes to matters of Torah, and Hashem will assist him (cf. *Tehillim* 81:11).

Chapter 47

Rabbah and Rav Yosef

In 4059 (299 C.E.), Rabbah became the leader of the Sages in Babylonia. The Sages were unsure whether it was better to appoint Rabbah, who was called the *"oker harim"* (he who moves mountains with his brilliant, analytical mind), or Rav Yosef ben Chiya, who was called "Sinai" (he who knows the entire Torah, both the oral and written law, as when it was received at Sinai). The Sages sought advice from the Sages in Eretz Yisrael, and they were told to choose Sinai. However, the question became academic because Rav Yosef refused to accept the position. Thus, Rabbah was chosen (*Berachos* 64a).

Rabbah was the leader for twenty-two years, until 4081 (321 C.E.). For these twenty-two years, Rav Yosef kept a low profile, so as not to interfere with Rabbah's authority (*Horayos* 14a).

Rabbah had four hundred full-time students and twelve thousand part-time students who came for twice yearly for month-long study sessions known as *yarchei kallah* (*Bava Metzia* 86a).

He passed away while proclaiming a halachic decision concerning ritual purity. A *bas kol* announced: "You are fortunate, for your body is pure and your soul has departed in purity" (ibid.).

After Rabbah passed away, Rav Yosef led the Sages in Babylonia for two and a half years.

Although he was blind, he knew the entire Torah perfectly.

He fasted forty days in order to remember his learning. He repeated the fasts so that his children should always learn Torah, and then repeated the fasts a third time so that his grandchildren should also continue in his ways (ibid. 85a).

One-minute history lesson: Because Rav Yosef displayed such humility in deferring to Rabbah, his own life was extended so that he would lead the Sages after Rabbah's passing.

There are many historical examples of people who practiced humility and merited extended life spans. This benefit alone speaks well for developing the trait of humility in ourselves.

Chapter 48

Abaye and Rava

A baye, an orphan from both parents, was raised by his uncle, the great Rabbah (see chapter 47). He was chosen to be the *nasi* in Pumbedisa, Babylonia, in 4084 (324 C.E.) and led for thirteen years. There were four candidates for *nasi* at the time: Abaye, Rava, Rav Zeira and Rabbah bar Masna. Each one was tested and Abaye did the best. This was considered a Heavenly sign that it was Abaye's turn to lead (*Horayos* 14a and *Rashi*).

Every week, on Shabbos, Abaye would receive a greeting from Heaven (*Taanis* 21b). This amazing occurrence demonstrated that he was chosen by Heaven to begin the immense task of arranging the *Talmud Bavli* (the Babylonian Talmud), which is the Torah guidebook and code of Jewish law forever (Rav Avigdor Miller, *Exalted People*, para. 660).

He was always God-fearing, gentle, peaceful, and accessible to all (*Berachos* 17a).

When Abaye passed away, Rava became the *nasi*

for fourteen years, from 4098 to 4112 (338 to 352 C.E.)

He always prayed to become as wise as Rav Huna (see chapter 46), wealthy as Rav Chisda (see chapter 46), and humble as Rabbah (see chapter 47) [*Moed Katan* 28a].

The whole *Talmud Bavli* is called the research of Abaye and Rava (*Sukkah* 28a). The *Talmud Yerushalmi*, on the other hand, was never sealed. Its arrangement stopped at the beginning of Rava's leadership due to persecutions in Eretz Yisrael.

When people would honor Rava, he would re-peat to himself a verse from *Iyov* (20:6–7): "Though he becomes great and rises to the clouds...yet he shall disappear and people will say, 'Where is he?' " (*Yoma* 87a).

He was greeted by Heaven once a year on Yom Kippur (*Taanis* 21b).

One-minute history lesson: Although Abaye was chosen to be the leader before Rava and he received a Heavenly greeting once a week, the halachah follows Rava in all but six cases (*Bava Metzia* 22b). Further, Rava's name appears in *Talmud Bavli* most frequently of all the Sages (Rav Avigdor Miller, *Exalted People*, para. 665).

We see from this that people can excel in different areas of life — some in Torah, some in *chesed*, and some in *avodah* (prayer). Just as Abaye and Rava each excelled in their own realms, we too must strive to develop our talents and become the greatest we can become. Hashem knows whether or not we are fulfilling our full, true potential. His rewards are commensurate with our efforts and the difficulties we overcome.

Chapter 49

Hillel II and the Calendar

In 4119 (359 C.E.), Hillel II, son of Rabbi Yehudah Nesiah III, arranged the Jewish calendar for all future generations. The Jewish calendar is based upon the Torah system of following the lunar year, but the natural seasons correspond to the solar year. The calendar designed by Hillel II instituted a system of leap years so that our calendar, based on the lunar months, which are twenty-nine and a half days long, would still match the Jewish holidays with their appointed seasons. If the leap years established by Hillel II were not followed, Pesach, which is to be observed in the spring, would come out in the wrong season.

In addition to instituting a system of leap years, the establishment of a calendar brought to a close the old system of how Rosh Chodesh, the first day of a lunar month, was identified. Up until the institution of the calendar system, a new month would not be recognized until witnesses who had seen the new moon came to testify before the Sages of the Sanhedrin (*Rosh HaShanah* 25b). In order to inform the people in all distant communities of the start of a new month, the Sages initially used fire signals from hilltops. When this method was discontinued, they used couriers, until they were unable to do that as well.

In the days of Abaye and Rava (see previous chapter), the Sages had already discontinued the practice of depending on witnesses. There was already a fixed calendar at that time, but they still required Beis Din to sanctify the new month (Rambam, *Hilchos Kiddush HaChodesh* 5:3).

The Sages then gathered under the authority of Hillel II to consecrate all the new moons and leap years for the future, until the Redemption, may it come speedily. This was the last Beis Din in Eretz Yisrael; thus, they took care of our nation's needs for the future. Afterwards, the Sanhedrin disbanded and the higher levels of closeness to Hashem ceased.

One-minute history lesson: We need to appreciate Hillel II and the Sages' great scholarship, which resulted in our perfect calendar. We are able to know when Rosh Chodesh is in our time because the Beis Din in Eretz Yisrael in 4119 (359 C.E.) designated this day as Rosh Chodesh for us. It is an amazing system that we should not take for granted.

Chapter 50

Rav Ashi and the Talmud Bavli

etween 4131 (371 C.E.) and 4187 (427 C.E.), Rav Ashi closed and sealed off the *Talmud Bavli* forever. Rav Ashi had studied under all of the great Sages of the generation, and he served as *nasi* for fifty-five years.

> *From the days of Rebbe until Rav Ashi, we do not find such Torah and greatness in one person.*
> (*Gittin* 59a)

For most of the time, Ravina (I) helped Rav Ashi and his yeshivah of Sages in finalizing the Talmud (*Bava Metzia* 86a). Rashi explains that this group of Sages were the end of the period of the *amoraim*; thus, they were able to organize all of the teachings in the present format.

The Rif explains at the end of *Maseches Eiruvin*

that the *Talmud Bavli* includes the information contained in the *Talmud Yerushalmi*, since the *Talmud Bavli* was completed after the *Talmud Yerushalmi*.

> *All Jews are obligated to follow all that is*
> *included in Talmud Bavli. These lessons are the*
> *conclusions of all the Sages or of their majority*
> *for all time.*
>
> (Rambam, Preface to *Yad HaChazakah*)

After the period of the *amoraim* (the Sages of the Gemara), the period of the *rabbanan savora'ei* (the Sages after the Gemara) began. It lasted from 4235 to 4349 (fifth to sixth century C.E.).

The Talmud was not put into actual written form until Rav Yosei of the *rabbanan savora'ei* era. He was the *rosh yeshivah* in Pumbedisa, Babylonia, for forty years, beginning in 4236 (476 C.E.).

One-minute history lesson: Although originally the oral law was not given in a written format, with the increased persecution of the Jews in exile, the Sages realized that it was essential to preserve the Torah in writing. The period of the *amoraim* in Babylonia was a relatively peaceful period, enabling the Sages to clarify many rulings and record all that they had learned. This was a great kindness from Hashem.

The prophet Yeshayah promises us, "The

Torah shall not depart from your children and grandchildren forever" (*Yeshayah* 59:21). In addition, the Midrash teaches:

Hashem always arranges yeshivos for the Jewish nation where they can study diligently, by day and by night. They immerse themselves in Torah study to clarify each topic thoroughly.... These places will manage to be exempt from persecution.... Hashem has mercy on the Jewish nation so that the Torah should not be forgotten....
(*Midrash Tanchuma, Noach* 3).

Part 6

Later Leaders in Babylonia

Chapter 51

The Good-Day Person

Mar, the son of Rav Ashi, would sign his name "Tav-Yomi," which means good day. He once overhead a fool saying, "The next *rosh yeshivah* will be the man who signs his name 'Tav-Yomi.' " Mar took the hint and traveled to the center of Jewish learning at that time, Masa Mechasya. His "name" was a result of his always focusing on the positive. His efforts in self-improvement helped him to make it a good day for himself and for our nation (*Bava Basra* 12b).

Mar served as *nasi* for thirteen years, from 4214 to 4227 (454 to 467 C.E.).

Mar said, "I love every scholar as myself" (*Shabbos* 119a).

We always follow Mar's halachic decisions with only two exceptions (*Rashi, Chullin* 76b).

It is interesting to note that Mar passed away right after Yom Kippur, which, in a sense, is the best day of the year — a day of atonement, forgiveness, and achieving closeness to Hashem.

> *One-minute history lesson:* Every day has the
> potential to be a "Tav-Yom." Think positive
> and allow Hashem to "lead you in the direction
> you desire to go" (*Makkos* 10b).
>
> Every day is a good day — if you don't
> agree, consider skipping one day!

Chapter 52

Rabbanan Savora'ei and the Geonim

The Sages who lived after the era of the *amoraim* are referred to as *savora'ei*. By that time, the Talmud was all in place. The word *savora'ei* is similar to the Aramaic word "*sevara*," understanding, for these Sages expounded on the Talmud with *sevara*, understanding and depth.

The era of the *savora'ei* lasted from approximately 4235 until 4349 (475 to 589 C.E.).

Beginning in 4236 (476 C.E.), Rabbi Yosef was Nasi. Rabbi Simona became leader in 4280 (520 C.E.).

The next era was that of the *geonim*. It lasted for approximately 450 years, from 4349 until 4798 (589 to 1038 C.E.). The first *gaon* in 4349 (589 C.E.) was Rabbi Chanan. The Sages who lived during this era knew all of *Shas* (all six sections of the Talmud) by heart (*Meiri*, Introduction to *Pirkei Avos*).

In 4510 (750 C.E.), Rav Yehudai Gaon wrote a *sefer* called *Halachos Pesukos*. He was blind, so he dictated the text of this work, which is also known as "*Re'u*," from the verse "See what Hashem has given you" (*Shemos* 16:29). This *sefer* teaches the concept of appreciating and understanding Hashem's kindness. (See *Doros HaRishonim* 4:20.)

Also in 4510, Rav Achai Gaon settled in Eretz Yisrael. He wrote the *Sheiltos*, halachah (Jewish law) and aggadah (parables containing many lessons) in a sequence following the weekly Torah portions.

In 4575 (815 C.E.), Rav Yosef Gaon became head of the yeshivah in Pumbedisa. He was such an outstanding scholar that it is said that Eliyahu HaNavi attended his lectures (*Iggeres Rav Sherira Gaon* 3:7).

From approximately 4613 to 4636 (853 to 876 C.E.), Rabbi Amram Gaon was the *rosh yeshivah* composed a siddur, putting the prayers into writing for the first time.

From 4631 to 4640 (871 to 880 C.E.), Rav Tzemach Gaon headed the yeshivah. He wrote *Sefer Aruch*, a Talmudic dictionary with novel insights and interpretations.

From 4642 to 4702 (882 to 942 C.E.), Rav Saadya Gaon was the *rosh yeshivah*. He wrote many *sefarim*, including *Emunos VeDei'os* on Jewish philosophy.

Rabbi Sherira Gaon and his son, Rabbi Hai

Gaon, were the last of the *geonim*. They each lived for almost one hundred years. Rabbi Sherira Gaon became leader in 4728 (968 C.E.). In 4746, he wrote his famous *Iggeres* (letter) of historical records, covering the periods of the *amoraim, savoraim*, and *geonim*. Rabbi Hai Gaon was leader from 4763 to 4798 (1003 to 1038 C.E.), about thirty-five years.

The story is told of a Jewish leader, Bustenai, a descendant of the family of David, who lived from 4378 to 4430 (618 to 670 C.E.). He became *reish galusa* (the head of the Jews in Babylonia) upon finding favor by the ruling caliph of that time. The caliph called upon Bustenai and was impressed by the manner in which Bustenai stood at attention in his presence, without moving, even when a fly landed on his forehead. When asked why he ignored the fly, Bustenai replied, "We have a tradition that when standing in the presence of a king, one does not speak, laugh, or budge without permission." His noble behavior found favor and he was appointed *reish galusa* (Rabbi Yechiel Halperin, *Seder HaDoros*, p. 284).

One-minute history lesson: Incredibly, Bustenai rose to become *reish galusa*, the leader of the Jewish people, with the assistance of an insect. The *Ramban* (on *Shemos* 13:16) teaches us that everything that happens to us is a result of Divine decree. Hashem can bring about

changes in circumstances from seemingly un-
likely occurrences. It is our task to learn from
these occurrences and be inspired to recognize
and serve Hashem.

Chapter 53

Four Captives

Sometime between 4715 (955 C.E.) and 4720 (960 C.E.), toward the end of the period of the *geonim*, an incident occurred that spread Torah to many corners of the world. Four great scholars from southern Italy were captured by pirates and eventually ransomed by Jewish communities across the Mediterranean. These captives were:

1. Rabbeinu Chushiel, who ended up in North Africa and established a yeshivah in Tunisia. He was the father of Rabbeinu Chananel and the teacher of Rabbeinu Nissim.

2. Rabbeinu Shemaryah, who was redeemed by the Jews of Alexandria, Egypt, and established a yeshivah there.

3. Rabbeinu Moshe. He and his son, Chanoch, ended up in Cordova, Spain, where he began a great yeshivah.

4. Rabbi Nassan, who went to France. (Some say the identity of the last captive is unknown).

One-minute history lesson: As Torah scholarship was declining in Babylonia, Hashem arranged for these four scholars to spread Torah to outlying Torah communities (*Doros HaRishonim* 4:302). Hashem has many ways of transmitting His Torah, making it available to Jewry all over.

Part 7

Rishonim

Chapter 54

Early Rishonim

Rabbeinu Gershom Meor HaGolah (the Light of the Diaspora) of France lived from 4720 to 4800 (960 to 1040 C.E.). His commentary to the Talmud is in the margin of many volumes of *Shas*. Of him, Rashi (Rabbi Shlomo Yitzchaki, the foremost commentator of the Chumash and Talmud) would later write: "We all live by his teachings." His disciples were Rashi's teachers. He is famous for the *takanos* (regulations) that he instituted, such as not to marry more than one wife.

Rabbeinu Chananel ben Chushiel became leader in North Africa in 4815 (1055 C.E.). His commentary to the Talmud can be found in many *masechtos* (volumes of the Talmud). The work of the Rif (Rabbi Yitzchak Alfasi) is based on Rabbeinu Chananel's commentary to the Talmud (*Rashba, Kesubos* 80b). Rabbeinu Chananel amassed amazing insights from his predecessors, which he passed on to later generations (*Chazon Ish, Bava Kama* 11:20).

The Rif lived from 4773 until 4863 (1013 to 1103 C.E.). His summary of halachos is in the back of most *masechtos*. He was a disciple of Rabbeinu Chananel ben Chushiel and Rabbeinu Nissim. Meiri (a French Talmudist) states that the Rif was the greatest halachic authority of that time. *Tosafos* states that the Divine Presence helped the Rif compose and arrange his work. It has been called the "*Talmud Katan*," the condensed form of the Talmud. It was used by the Beis Yosef (see chapter 64) as one of the three pillars of the *Shulchan Aruch*, along with the Rambam (see chapter 56) and the Rosh (see chapter 60).

> *One-minute history lesson:* Although the To-rah does permit a man to marry more than one wife and we even have examples of people doing this, such as Avraham Avinu and Yaakov Avinu, the Sages are authorized by the Torah to institute regulations like the "*Cherem* of Rabbeinu Gershon" when they see that it is necessary. This principle has been followed throughout our history to this day. The vision and insight of our Sages guide us in fulfilling the Torah in every situation that may develop.

Chapter 55

Rashi and Rabbeinu Bachya

Rashi (Rabbi Shlomo Yitzchaki), the foremost commentator of the Talmud, lived from 4800 to 4865 (1040 to 1105 C.E.). Thus, the Rif (see previous chapter) was twenty-seven years old when Rashi was born. The Rif was considered the greatest scholar in Sephardic traditions, while Rashi became the greatest scholar in Askenazic traditions.

Whenever you open a *sefer* of *Nach*, or a *gemara*, the commentary of Rashi is there. Rashi's commentary is the one that opens our eyes to understanding the text.

The Rosh (Rabbi Asher ben Yechiel of Barcelona, Spain) tells us in *Orchos Chaim* (2:11) to be as precise as possible in analyzing every word of Rashi.

The Shelah HaKadosh (Rabbi Yeshayahu HaLevi Horowitz) says that there are many deep ideas hidden in Rashi's words, which were written with *ruach hakodesh* (Divine inspiration).

Rashi had three daughters. All of them married great Sages, Rabbi Meir, the Rivan, and Rabbeinu Efrayim, who all became authors of *Tosafos*.

The Chida (Rabbi Chaim Yosef David Azulai) says that Rashi fasted for 613 days before writing his commentary to the Chumash.

*   *   *

Rabbeinu Bachya, who lived approximately from 4760 to 4826 (1000 to 1066 C.E.), is primarily known by his most famous work, *Chovos HaLevavos* (Duties of the Heart).

Just as Rashi is basic to understanding every Torah text, *Chovos HaLevavos*, written about the same time as Rashi wrote his commentaries, is basic to understanding the ethical foundations of Judaism.

It is said that an angel, called a *maggid*, told Rabbi Yosef Caro to study a portion of *Chovos HaLevavos* daily.

The Chasam Sofer (Rabbi Moshe Sofer of Frankfurt-am-Main) would teach his students from this work for fifteen minutes before every lecture.

Rav Avigdor Miller, *zt"l*, said: "If you want to be a happy person, learn *Chovos HaLevavos*."

One-minute history lesson: In his commentary to *Berachos* (25b), Rabbi Akiva Eiger lists about forty-five places in *Shas* where Rashi raises a question and answers, "I don't know." This teaches us the unique greatness of Rashi, who always fulfilled the *mishnah* in *Avos* (5:10): "A wise person always admits the truth." Rather than skip over those questions, Rashi admitted when he had no answers.

This trait has been pointed out as a key to Rashi's stature. Because he admitted to his lack of knowledge in a few places, we realize that in all other places Rashi knew everything with perfect clarity, since if not he would have mentioned his uncertainty.

Chapter 56

Rambam and
Rabbeinu Tam

The Rambam, Rabbi Moshe ben Maimon, lived from 4895 to 4968 (1135 to 1208 C.E.). The Chida said of him: "From Moshe Rabbeinu until Moshe ben Maimon there was no one else to compare to Moshe Rabbeinu."

It has also been said that verse 4,895 of the Torah, "Moshe began to explain the Torah," (*Devarim* 1:5), alludes to the Rambam, who was born in the year 4895.

Indeed, one of the Rambam's most famous works, the *Mishneh Torah*, means an "explanation" or "review of the Torah." The *Mishneh Torah* is an amazing work, codifying the entire *Shas* into fourteen divisions in a very systematic and concise manner. For this reason it is called the "*Yad*" (which has a numerical value of fourteen in Hebrew).

Even the Raavad, who occasionally criticizes the Rambam's decisions, writes that the Rambam's codification of the entire Torah was a great achievement (Raavad, *Hilchos Kilayim* 10).

Seder HaDoros (p. 341) relates that the Ramban had difficulty understanding Torah as a youngster, but he persevered until at some point his mind began to develop and he went to learn from Rabbi Yosef Ibn Migash, where he became known as a great genius. The night after the Rambam concluded his great work, his father appeared to him in a dream with another person, whom his father introduced as Moshe Rabbeinu, saying, "He came to congratulate you on your masterpiece."

*   *   *

Rabbi Yaakov ben Meir, known as Rabbeinu Tam, lived from 4860 until 4931 (1100 to 1171 C.E.). He was a grandson of Rashi (see previous chapter).

He is called "Tam" because the Torah refers to Yaakov Avinu as *"Yaakov ish tam"* (*Bereishis* 25:27) — a perfect individual who spent his time in places of Torah.

Rabbeinu Tam's teachings on *Shas* are all over the Talmud, incorporated in *Tosafos*, the additions to Rashi's commentary.

He had two brothers: Rivam, Rabbi Yitzchak ben Rabbi Meir, and Rashbam, Rabbi Shmuel ben Rabbi Meir, both of whom are also quoted frequently in

Tosafos. Rashbam also has a commentary on *Bava Basra* and on the last chapter of *Pesachim*. He also wrote a commentary on the Torah, which focuses on the *peshat*, the literal explanation of each verse.

One-minute history lesson: The Rambam is credited with formulating the Thirteen Principles of Faith, which are printed at the end of the morning prayers in our siddurim.

The first of these principles is: "I believe with perfect faith that the Creator, Blessed is His Name, created and guides all things and that He alone did, does, and will control everything." This and all the rest of the principles contain a wealth of information. They are the Torah concepts we live by.

The *Alei Shur* (1:158) writes that in order for one to develop an advanced level of self-knowledge, it is essential to study four basic Torah works: 1) The Rambam's *Hilchos Dei'os* and *Shemoneh Perakim*, 2) *Chovos HaLevavos*, 3) Rabbeinu Yonah's *Shaarei Teshuvah* and his commentary on *Mishlei*, and 4) *Ohr Yisrael* by Rav Yitzchak Blazer.

Chapter 57

Baalei HaTosafos

"*Baalei HaTosafos*" is the name given to the many Sages who gave us the various *Tosafos* teachings we have today. "These scholars were the ones who unified *Shas* by connecting all the related topics, showing us how to understand the similarities and differences of the texts" (*Yam Shel Shlomo*, Introduction to *Chullin*).

Rabbeinu Yitzchak ben Rabbi Shmuel (the Ri), who lived from 4880 to 4960 (1120 to 1200 C.E.), was the son of Rabbeinu Tam's sister. (See previous chapter about Rabbeinu Tam.)

The Ri led sixty scholars who learned together. Each scholar knew all of *Shas* and in addition knew one *masechta* by heart. For each lesson, they would all examine the material carefully from all angles so that their interpretation would fit with all of the other teachings throughout *Shas* (*Seder HaDoros* 350).

The Ri's name appears frequently in *Tosafos*, almost as often as Rabbeinu Tam's does.

The Rishonim (ArtScroll History Series [New York: Mesorah Publications, 1982], p. 157) lists fifty-three of the *baalei haTosafos.*

> *One-minute history lesson:* The underlying goals of Rashi's commentary (to explain the basic meaning and lesson of each phrase) and *Tosafos* (the additional lessons on the Gemara) are symbolic of our purpose in this world. We need to keep practicing the basics while at the same time striving to add to our achievements and to take spiritual strides.

Chapter 58

Kuzari and Ibn Ezra

Rabbi Yehudah HaLevi, who lived from 4840 to 4905 (1080 to 1145 C.E.), wrote *The Kuzari*, a fundamental *sefer* on the basics of Judaism, written in dialogue. The Vilna Gaon praises *The Kuzari* highly. *Seder HaDoros* writes that it is filled with wisdom which we should learn and teach to our children and students.

Rabbi Yehudah HaLevi also composed the Shabbos song *Yom Shabbason*. His first name, Yehudah, is spelled out by the first letter of each stanza.

He is quoted often in the Ibn Ezra's commentary to the *Chumash*.

*   *   *

Rabbi Avraham Ibn Ezra, known as the Ibn Ezra, lived from 4849 to 4924 (1089 to 1164 C.E.).

He wrote a commentary on *Tanach*. In addition, he is mentioned in three places in *Tosafos* in *Shas*: *Rosh HaShanah* 13a, *Taanis* 20b, and *Kiddushin* 37b.

The Rambam encouraged his son in a letter to study the works of the Ibn Ezra.

One-minute history lesson: The Shabbos song *Yom Shabbason* has the following chorus: "On [Shabbos] the dove found rest, and on [Shabbos] we rest from exhaustion." The dove is used in Torah literature to represent the Jewish people, for like the dove, the Jewish people has only one mate, the *Ribbono shel Olam*.

These great Sages, each in his own way, taught us to serve Hashem and live our lives according to the Torah's guidelines.

Chapter 59

Ramban and Rabbeinu Yonah

R abbi Moshe ben Nachman, the Ramban, lived from 4954 to 5030 (1194 to 1270 C.E.). He wrote on the entire Chumash, on many *masechtos* of *Shas*, and many other works. The well-known *Iggeres HaRamban* is a letter he wrote to his son that contains directives for success in life.

The Rashba, Rabbi Shlomo Ibn Aderes, writes that the Ramban was the greatest in that generation in wisdom and fear of sin (*Responsa* 1:613).

The Rivash (Rabbi Yitzchak ben Sheshes Perfet), who lived in the Ramban's generation, writes that the Ramban was relied upon in his generation as we rely on Moshe Rabbeinu.

Many of the Ramban's writings are devoted to defending earlier Torah authorities. He writes: "Whoever separates himself from the teachings of our earlier Sages is like giving up his life. We need to always judge them [the Sages] favorably..." (*Milchemes Hashem* at the conclusion of *Rosh HaShanah*).

His commentary on the *Chumash* is praised by the Chasam Sofer for teaching the basic foundations of our faith (*Teshuvos* 1:61).

The Ramban taught: "The purpose of life is to believe in Hashem and to thank Him for creating us" (*Ramban*, *Shemos* 13:16).

*　　*　　*

Rabbeinu Yonah lived from 4940 until 5023 (1180 to 1263 C.E.). The Rashbatz (Rabbi Shimon Duran) wrote that there was none like him to draw people to the fear of Hashem and piety.

Rabbeinu Yonah is best known for authoring *Shaarei Teshuvah* (the Gates of Repentance), which many people study all year round, and especially during the month of Elul. The Chida writes of this *sefer*: "Fortunate is one who learns it daily to inspire a person to holiness and repentance." Rabbi Shimon Shkop, *zt"l*, was known to study this work for half an hour a day for fifty years of his life.

The Chafetz Chaim (Rabbi Yisrael Meir HaKohen Kagan) writes in the preface to *Sefer Chafetz Chaim* that *Shaarei Teshuvah* is a great work of *mussar* that deals with halachic criteria.

Rabbeinu Yonah's *sefer* on *Mishlei* is also praised highly.

One-minute history lesson: In history, as in our daily lives, Hashem enables us to interact with our teachers and friends in ways that are beneficial to our growth. There are many *sefarim* of the past and present that we can learn from as teachers.

Accept upon yourself a mentor, acquire for yourself a friend.
(*Avos* 1:6)

In his *sefer Alei Shur*, Rav Shlomo Wolbe (vol. 1, p. 29) teaches us that in order to acquire the basic foundations of Torah Judaism today, every Jewish student should study four basic works: 1) *Shulchan Aruch* with *Mishnah Berurah*, 2) *Chumash* with the commentaries of Rashi and Ramban, 3) *Pirkei Avos* with the commentary of Rabbeinu Yonah, and 4) *Mesilas Yesharim*.

Chapter 60

Rashba, Rosh, and Baal HaTurim

The Rashba, Rabbi Shlomo Ibn Aderes, lived from 4995 to 5070 (1235 to 1310 C.E.). He was a disciple of Ramban and Rabbeinu Yonah (see previous chapter).

He wrote more than ten thousand halachic responsa and is quoted extensively in the *Shulchan Aruch* (the Code of Jewish Law).

We have his *chiddushim* (novel insights) on seventeen tractates of the Talmud.

Some of his great disciples were Ritva (Rabbi Yom Tov Ibn Asevilli), Rabbeinu Bachya (author of a commentary on Chumash), and the Migdal Oz (author of a commentary on the Rambam).

*　　　*　　　*

The Rosh, Rabbi Asher ben Yechiel, lived from 5010 to 5088 (1250 to 1328 C.E.). He had eight sons who were all very learned. His halachic rulings are based on the words of the Rif (see chapter 54), and also include the insights of Rashi, *Tosafos*, and Rambam.

Rabbi Yosef Caro, who wrote the *Beis Yosef* and the *Shulchan Aruch*, writes that the Rosh is one of the three pillars of halachah from whom he draws his halachic conclusions in the *Shulchan Aruch*.

The Rosh also wrote an excellent *sefer* of brief guidelines on how to live successfully, known as *Orchos Chaim* (Pathways to Life) of the Rosh.

*   *   *

Rabbeinu Yaakov, the Baal HaTurim, was the third son of the Rosh. He lived from 5030 to 5103 (1270 to 1343 C.E.) and was born on the day that the Ramban died.

Rabbeinu Yaakov was known as the "Baal HaTurim" because he divided Jewish law into four *turim* (rows or volumes). These four volumes of Jewish law are:

1. *Orach Chaim* (laws of daily life)

2. *Yoreh Dei'ah* (laws of general prohibitions and commandments)

3. *Even HaEzer* (laws of marriage)

4. *Choshen Mishpat* (legal issues)

In addition to the *Arba'ah Turim*, the Baal HaTurim wrote two commentaries on Chumash, which are known as the *Baal HaTurim on Chumash*. The commentary printed in most editions of *Mikraos Gedolos* is the shorter one, which teaches amazing Torah insights based, in part, on *gematrios* (the numerical values of words) and the number of times a phrase is repeated in Tanach.

One-minute history lesson: It is worthwhile to review some selections from the Rosh's *sefer* for daily living:

- "Avoid idle talk. Be careful to study Torah at night until you fall asleep, rather than falling asleep while engaging in idle talk" (*Orchos Chaim* 1:18).

- "When the time for prayer arrives, set aside all your involvements and pray. Keep your eyes away from that which is not yours" (ibid., 20).

- "Trust Hashem with your whole heart. Believe in Hashem's Divine Providence and in His perfect Oneness. He is always watching you and supervising your actions..." (ibid., 26).

- "Don't trust in money for that is the start of idol worship. Spend money generously in fulfillment of [Hashem's] instructions for He can always replenish your supply and sustain your actions" (ibid. 2:3).

Chapter 61

Ran, Rivash, and Rashbatz

Rabbi Nissim ben Reuven, the Ran, lived from 5050 until 5141 (1290 to 1381). He wrote a commentary on the Rif (Rabbi Yitzchak Alfasi, see Chapter 54) for fourteen *masechtos*. In *Maseches Nedarim*, his commentary appears in the margin of the Gemara. We also have a collection of his *derashos* (lectures) on many topics.

His disciple, the Rivash writes (*siman 375*) that the Ran was the greatest Sage of his generation, far above all the other great leaders of the time.

The Nimukei Yosef, another disciple of the Ran, also wrote a commentary on the Rif.

The Maggid Mishneh, a colleague of the Ran, wrote a commentary by this name on the Rambam.

*   *   *

The Rivash, Rabbi Yitzchak ben Sheshes Perfet,

lived from 5086 to 5169 (1326 to 1409 C.E.). He was considered the "*chad bedoro*," the unique great one of his generation (*Tashbeitz* 160).

The Mabit, Rabbi Moshe Trani, states (*Teshuvah* 280) that the Rivash was the authority on halachah, just like Rabbi Nachman in his generation of the Sages of the Talmud.

The Beis Yosef says that we rely on the Responsa of the Rivash even more than on others of his time.

*   *   *

The Rashbatz, a disciple of the Rivash, lived from 5121 to 5204 (1361 to 1444 C.E.). He wrote fourteen *sefarim*, including three volumes of Responsa on about eight hundred topics.

One-minute history lesson: Starting from 5235 (1475 C.E.), about twenty-five years after the invention of the printing press, Jewish *sefarim* began to appear in printed form. Until this time people used to copy over *sefarim* by hand, which was a time-consuming process. Since it was done with determination to study Torah, Hashem assisted them with inventions to make the work easier.

"On the path one is determined to go, he will be led" (*Makkos* 10b.) When we focus on an objective, Hashem will help us succeed.

Chapter 62

Torah Commentators of the Fifteenth Century

In 5252 (1492 C.E.), the Jews were expelled from Spain. Don Yitzchak Abarbanel, known as the Abarbanel, who lived from 5197 to 5268 (1437 to 1508 C.E.), was the king's finance minister and was invited by the king to stay. He made a plea that the decree of expulsion be rescinded. However, his plea was not accepted, and he chose to join his brethren in exile.

Although he lost his great fortune and powerful position, Abarbanel himself writes that he benefitted from the expulsion because he had been so occupied in the king's palace that he had had little time to devote himself to Torah. After the expulsion, he was able to continue his commentary on Tanach and write on *Pirkei Avos*, the Haggadah, and philosophy.

The Beis Yosef called him the "great eagle" (*Shulchan Aruch, Orach Chaim* 168).

*   *   *

Rabbi Ovadyah of Bartenura, known as the Bartenura, lived from 5210 to 5270 (1450 to 1510 C.E.). He is famous for his commentary on the Mishnah. His commentary is called "the Rav," based on the acronym of his name. He explains even difficult *mishnayos* in a clear style and thus has become everyone's rebbe.

*   *   *

Rabbi Yaakov Ibn Chaviv lived from 5205 to 5276 (1445 to 1516 C.E.) and is famous for producing a collection of the *aggadata* (stories and lessons) sections of the Gemara. He is known by the name of his commentary, the *Ein Yaakov*. In addition to the *aggadatas* as found in the Gemara, the commentary consists of the thoughts of earlier Sages and Rabbi Yaakov's own insights.

One-minute history lesson: The Abarbanel was able to develop his Torah thoughts more fully as a result of the Spanish Expulsion, even though it was a terrible event for the Jewish people. Throughout our expulsions and sufferings, the Jewish people has been busy perfecting itself. Hashem sends various forms of "wake-up calls" to prompt us to growth and awareness. The Torah way is to always strive to delve deeper into Torah study, mitzvah application, and self-improvement.

Chapter 63

The Radvaz, the Shitah, and the Ari

Rabbi David Ibn Avi Zimra, the Radvaz, lived from 5240 to 5335 (1480 to 1575 C.E.).

His responsa (written responses to inquiries on halachah) of about three thousand *teshuvos* include about seventy responsa that were transmitted by Heavenly inspiration (*ruach hakodesh*).

He also wrote a commentary on many sections of the Rambam's *Mishneh Torah*.

*　　　*　　　*

Rabbi Betzalel Ashkenazi, who wrote the *Shitah Mekubetzes*, lived from 5280 until 5352 (1520 to 1592 C.E.). The *Shitah Mekubetzes*, a collection of insights by many great *rishonim* on many *masechtos*, is his most famous work. It is used to this day in yeshivos all over the world.

Rabbi Betzalel was a disciple of the Radvaz. His

notes on *Maseches Kodashim* appear in the margins of the Gemara.

*   *   *

Rabbi Yitzchak Luria Ashkenazi, the Ari HaKadosh, known as the "Ari," or the "Arizal," lived from 5294 to 5332 (1534 to 1572 C.E.). He was a disciple of the Shitah and the Radvaz and a great Kabbalist.

The Beis Yosef said that his *neshamah* (soul) was as great as that of a prophet.

At the age of thirty-six, the Arizal moved to Tzefas. He soon became the head of the Kabbalists there. He developed a new approach to Kabbalah, which his major disciple, Rabbi Chaim Vital, recorded in *Eitz Chaim*. Rabbi Chaim Vital writes that the Arizal once told him that he had just learned a most amazing topic which would take him more than eighty years of nonstop teaching to transmit (*Pri Eitz Chaim* p. 156).

The Vilna Gaon spoke of the Ari's knowledge of the hidden secrets of Torah and of his meetings with Eliyahu the Prophet. He used to tremble when he spoke of the Arizal.

One-minute history lesson: One of the Arizal's famous teachings is "Before praying in the morning, one should accept upon himself the mitzvah, 'Love your fellow Jew as yourself' (*Vayikra* 19:18)." Besides being a great mitzvah, this reminds us to have our fellow Jews in mind in our prayers.

Part 8

Acharonim

Chapter 64

Rabbi Yosef Caro

Rabbi Yosef Caro, known as the Beis Yosef, lived from 5248 to 5335 (1488 to 1575 C.E.). The number 248 is a hint that he would teach Jewry how to sustain its 248 limbs. This fits with Rabbi Yosef's introduction to his *sefer Beis Yosef*, where he explains that he called his work *Beis Yosef* because Yosef HaTzaddik was the sustainer of all of Jewry in Egypt.

The *Beis Yosef* is an elaborate commentary to the *Tur* (see chapter 60). Rabbi Yosef later condensed this work into the *Shulchan Aruch*, which is his most famous work. *Shulchan Aruch* literally means "the Set Table," but it is commonly known as "The Code of Jewish Law." Following the system of the *Tur*, it divides Jewish law into four sections, and it includes references from the Talmud, Rashi, *Tosafos*, Ran, Rif, Rosh, Rambam, Rashba, Rivash, and many more.

The era of the *Shulchan Aruch* has been described as the transition period between the *rishonim* and the *acharonim*. It consolidated the work of those from before and became the focal point for the Sages that followed.

The Chida writes in *Shem HaGedolim* that there were three great leaders of Rabbi Yosef's generation who could have produced such a work as the Beis Yosef. However, Rabbi Yosef was the one who merited to write it because of his exceptional humility.

Rabbi Yosef also wrote *Kesef Mishneh*, a commentary on the Rambam's *Mishneh Torah*.

The Shelah HaKadosh writes that the three great leaders of his generation, Rabbi Yosef Caro, Rabbi Moshe Cordovero, and the Ari HaKadosh (see previous chapter), were all like angels.

Rabbi Yosef also wrote *Maggid Meisharim*, ethical lessons that he had been taught by an angel.

One-minute history lesson: Humility is the hallmark of the Torah leaders of our nation (*Chullin* 89a). We need to realize that, in our personal lives also, the more we develop ourselves in this area, the more we will succeed in every area.

Our greatest leader, Moshe Rabbeinu, was the most humble person who ever lived (*Bemidbar* 12:3). That is why he achieved the status of the greatest prophet in history.

It is important to note that although the Beis Yosef intended the *Shulchan Aruch* to be the final word on halachah, many commentaries have been written on it and many more books of halachah have been produced since its publication. The system of learning *Shas* through questions and answers, proofs and analyses, is a system that keeps the Torah alive in every generation. Because customs change and new situations develop, there is no such thing as a *sefer* that is a final word on any topic. In every generation, we apply the Torah guidelines from Sinai to our lives anew.

Chapter 65

The Rama and the Maharal of Prague

Rabbi Moshe Isserles, the Rama, lived from 5290 to 5332 (1530 to 1572 C.E.).

The *Shulchan Aruch*, written by the Beis Yosef (see previous chapter), was based mainly on the great Sephardic authorities. To provide practical halachic guidelines for Jews of Ashkenazic descent, the Rama wrote a *sefer* entitled *Darkei Moshe*, a commentary on the *Tur* which focuses on sources from the Ashkenazic Sages, such as Rashi and *Tosafos*. The Rama also wrote additions to the *Shulchan Aruch*, which appear in the text of the *Shulchan Aruch*.

Of the Rama, the Maharshal says: "From Moshe [Rabbeinu] and from Moshe ben Maimon [the Rambam] until Moshe [Isserles] there were none like you."

Although the Rama occasionally disagreed with the final ruling of the Beis Yosef, he wrote about him, "All those who disagree with you are as one who argues with the *Shechinah* [Divine presence]" (Responsa 48).

*   *   *

Rabbi Yehudah Loewe, the Maharal of Prague, lived from about 5272 to 5369 (1512 to 1609 C.E.).

A profound and prolific author, the Maharal wrote *Gur Aryeh*, a commentary on Rashi's commentary to the Chumash; *Gevuros Hashem* on the Exodus; *Netzach Yisrael* on the World to Come and Mashiach; and many more. His writing is characterized by deep thinking and analysis of the *aggadatas*.

The author of *Tosafos Yom Tov* (a commentary on the Mishnah), Rabbi Yom Tov Lipman Heller, was a disciple of the Maharal. He wrote his work as a result of his rebbe's emphasis on the study of *mishnayos*.

The Maharal was well versed in Kabbalah, and he is also famous for his connection to the Golem of Prague.

One-minute history lesson: The Rama was a great teacher of halachah, and the Maharal was a great teacher of *aggadata*. We see that in every generation, Hashem provides us with a balance of leaders of different aproaches to guide each Jewish community according to its needs.

Chapter 66

Gifts to Jewry

abbi Shmuel Edels, the Maharsha, lived from 5315 to 5392 (1555 to 1632 C.E.). His commentary on the Talmud is printed in the back of most Gemaras. Many Sages have emphasized the importance of studying this commentary. The Chazon Ish writes that it is essential for a deeper comprehension of Gemara, Rashi, and *Tosafos* (*Kovetz Iggros* 1:1).

The Bach praises the Maharsha highly in his Responsa (no. 43).

Many say that his words were written with *ruach hakodesh*.

The Chazon Ish (*Kovetz Iggros* 1:1) states that the Maharsha's commentary on the Talmud was a gift that Hashem provided for the Jewish nation. It helps train a person to toil in Torah study, which elevates and transforms a person. It also helps one to remember his studies better. The great *gaon* Rabbi Akiva Eiger studied all of the Maharsha's teachings.

In *Bava Basra* (10b), we find: "Fortunate are those who come here [the World to Come] prepared with their learning in hand." The Maharsha explains, "One who writes down and records his Torah insights will be fortunate."

*   *   *

Rabbi Yom Tov Lipman Heller, the Tosafos Yom Tov, lived from 5339 to 5414 (1579 to 1654 C.E.). He wrote the *Tosafos Yom Tov* on the Mishnah, which helps explain the Rav's more concise commentary.

He also wrote commentaries to the Rosh (see chapter 60) on *Shas* and divided the *Orchos Chaim* of the Rosh into a seven-day program so that it would be studied in the synagogue on a daily basis.

He instituted a special *"Mi Shebeirach"* to bless those who are careful to refrain from talking in shul.

One-minute history lesson: The history of our nation goes back farther than the history of any other nation. In the early seventeenth century, when Europeans were only beginning to settle in North America, Jews all over the world were busy developing their Torah skills. We learn from Rav Saadya Gaon, "We are the Torah nation," for, as we say in our daily prayers, "that is our life and the length of our days."

Chapter 67

Halachic Commentators

T he Bach, Rabbi Yoel Sirkis, lived from 5321 to 5400 (1561 to 1640 C.E.). In his commentary, the *Bayis Chadash*, he analyzes and explains the *Tur* (see chapter 60) and the *Beis Yosef* (see chapter 64).

He also wrote short, marginal corrections on all of *Shas*.

*   *   *

Rabbi David HaLevi Segal was a disciple of the Bach and became his son-in-law. Rabbi David is known as the Taz, which is the acronym of his *sefer*, *Turei Zahav*.

The Taz lived from 5346 to 5427 (1586 to 1667 C.E.). He wrote on the *Shulchan Aruch*, explaining the *Tur*, the *Beis Yosef*, and the *Bach*.

A woman whose son was very ill once came to the Taz, begging him to save her son's life. He said, "What can I do?" She insisted that his Torah study could help her. To this he replied, "The merits of my learning now should be a gift to your child." The child recovered (Rabbi Chaim Volozhiner, *Ruach Chaim* on *Avos* 1:1).

In *Yoreh Dei'ah* (251:6), the Taz writes: "It is more meritorious to study Torah and not have to be occupied with saving lives than to take away time from Torah to save a life. Torah study is the greatest of all mitzvos. However, one is obligated to interrupt his study to fulfill a mitzvah that cannot be done by others. Thus, if [one sees] someone who is, *chas veshalom*, drowning, and he is the only one available to save the person, he is obligated to do so."

The Pnei Yehoshua (Rabbi Yaakov Yehoshua Falk, 1680 to 1754 C.E.), writes in his approbation to the *Turei Zahav* that the halachah follows the opinion of the Taz in most places and that the Taz was the greatest of the later Sages.

*   *   *

The Shach, Rabbi Shabsai HaKohen, lived from 5382 to 5423 (1622 to 1663 C.E.).

He, too, wrote a commentary to the *Shulchan Aruch*, which is called *Sifsei Kohen*. In his introduction, he explains that he spent much effort and exertion on his commentary and that he clarified each point carefully many times, even one hundred and one times, in order to do his best to avoid making an error that would mislead someone.

*   *   *

The Magen Avraham, Rabbi Avraham Gombiner, lived from 5394 to 5442 (1634 to 1682 C.E.). He is the author of *Magen Avraham*, a commentary on the *Orach Chaim* section of the *Shulchan Aruch*.

Rabbi Zalman Volozhiner, whose story is told in the *sefer Toldos Adom*, writes that the Magen Avraham was regarded as a *rishon*, someone who lived in the earlier generations.

The Pri Megadim (Rabbi Yosef Teomim, 1712–1792 C.E.) writes that the Magen Avraham achieved the level of studying Torah *lishmah*, purely for its own sake.

He knew all of *mishnayos* by heart.

One-minute history lesson: There is always more that can be done in clarifying and teaching Torah concepts. There is no shortage of commentaries on halachah and they all enhance our learning in a different way.

Chapter 68

The Founder of Chassidus

Rabbi Yisrael ben Eliezer, who lived from 5460 to 5520 (1700 to 1760 C.E.), was called the Baal Shem Tov, "Master of a Good Name," for his unique style of behavior and leadership. He was the founder of Chassidus, a movement which changed the face of Eastern European Jewry.

He is known for secluding himself for long periods in forests and on mountains in order to study Torah, pray, meditate on the wonders of Creation and on man's relationship with Hashem.

When he was thirty-six, he began to mingle more with people to teach them his profound thoughts and to help even "simple" Jews.

He was orphaned at a young age. His father's last words were always in his mind: "Remember, Hashem is always with you, don't be afraid!"

He always emphasized loving every Jew and doing mitzvos with joy and song.

The Baal Shem Tov taught many disciples. One of these was Rabbi Dov Ber, the Maggid of Mezritch, who became the leader of Chassidus after the Baal Shem Tov's passing. Rabbi Dov Ber lived from 1704 to 1773 C.E., and taught many students.

The following is a list of some of the many Chassidic personalities who followed in the footsteps of the Baal Shem Tov:

- Rabbi Nachman of Breslov, a great-grandson of the Baal Shem Tov, who lived from 1772 to 1811 C.E. He authored *Likutei Moharan* and taught his disciples to serve Hashem with pure faith and joy.

- Rav Nachum of Chernobyl, who lived from 1730 to 1798 C.E.

- Rav Aharon of Karlin, founder of the Karlin-Stolin dynasty, who lived from 1736 to 1772. He is famous for his humility, for bringing many to repentance, and for praying with great devotion and love.

- Rabbi Shneur Zalman Schneerson, founder of Chabad Chassidus, who lived from 1745 to 1813. He wrote the *Tanya* and *Shulchan Aruch HaRav*, which is quoted extensively throughout the *Mishnah Berurah*. It is said that his name, *Shneur*, can be read *Shnei ur*, two lights, as a hint to his two works, which brought great light into the world (*Gedolei HaDoros*, p. 416).

- Rav Elimelech of Lizhensk, who lived from 1717 to 1786 C.E. He is the author of *No'am Elimelech*, a principal work of Chassidus which focuses on the weekly Torah portions. In addition, he was an extremely humble taddik. The Baal HaTanya said about him, "If someone would push him down, he would accept it with complete humilty."

- Rav Zusha of Anipoli, younger brother of Rav Elimelech, who lived from 1718 to 1800 C.E. For years the two brothers traveled around together as poor individuals, mingling with the multitudes to help bring Jews to Torah and mitzvos.

- Rabbi Levi Yitzchak of Berditchev, who lived from 1740 to 1810 C.E. He wrote *Kedushas Levi* on the Torah. In addition, he emphasized performing mitzvos with excitement and enthusiasm and loving every Jew and judging them in the most favorable way. He would defend his fellow Jews in the most amazing ways.

There are many *sefarim* and books that deal at length with these great personalities and their teachings.

One-minute history lesson: The Torah traditions have been transmitted from rebbe to disciple throughout the ages. There are as many chains of transmission as there are varieties of Jews in the Jewish nation. The Chassidim, the Litvaks, the Sephardim, the Yemenites, and all other groups all have their teachers, customs, and lessons of greatness.

Why did Hashem design the Jewish nation with so many diverse groups, similar in a sense to the twelve tribes, which were all different?

Rav Avigdor Miller, *zt"l*, says that we can also ask, "Why did Hashem create so many types of apples?" (*Or Olam*, vol. 10. p. 270). The answer is that it is for our benefit, to make life more enjoyable and meaningful.

The same can be said about the different groups in the Jewish nation. We learn from all groups. Whether we are Litvish, Chassidish, Sephardi, or Yemenite, the goal is to serve Hashem to the best of our abilities.

Chapter 69

The Ramchal

Rabbi Moshe Chaim Luzzato, known as the "Ramchal" (the acronym of his name), lived from 5467 to 5507 (1707 to 1747 C.E.). A brilliant Torah scholar and Kabbalist, he wrote *Mesilas Yesharim* ("The Path of the Righteous"), *Derech Hashem* ("The Way of Hashem"), *Daas Tevunos* ("The Knowing Heart"), *Derech Tevunos* ("The Ways of Reason"), and many other *sefarim*.

The Vilna Gaon says that in the first eight chapters of *Mesilas Yesharim*, there is not one extra word. The Vilna Gaon further stated: "If the Ramchal was still alive, I would go to study from him."

The Manchester *rosh yeshivah*, Rabbi Yehudah Zev Segal, *zt"l* (1910 to 1993 C.E.), studied *Mesilas Yesharim* regularly and lived by it his whole life. He once said, "Each time I learn [from this *sefer*] I experience a feeling of accomplishment" (*The Manchester Rosh Yeshiva* [New York: Mesorah Publications, 1997], p. 260).

Rabbi Yisrael Salanter said that his rebbe, Reb Zundel, told him that all *mussar sefarim* are good to study, but *Mesilas Yesharim* is the best guide. It teaches us our purpose in life and how to achieve it.

The *Alei Shur* (vol. 1, p. 30) writes that the "dictionary" for all character training is *Mesilas Yesharim*. It teaches us how to think in order to grow to perfection.

The *Alei Shur* cautions that although the words may seem simplistic, the more we study them the more we will discover their profoundness. Rabbi Yerucham Levovitz, the Mir *mashgiach*, *zt"l*, would say that *Mesilas Yesharim* contains, in a condensed form, all of the teachings of Kabbalah from all of the other *sefarim* of the Ramchal.

One-minute history lesson: *Mesilas Yesharim* teaches us many important Torah principles, including:

- "A person was created to have pleasure from Hashem."

- "The closer we come to Hashem, the more we perfect ourselves."

- "A person should draw close to Hashem like metal is drawn to a magnet."

- "External enthusiasm arouses one's inner feelings."

We need to review the *Mesilas Yesharim* regularly. The secret to success is to always review and apply the principles of success.

Chapter 70

The Vilna Gaon and His Legacy

R av Eliyahu, the Gaon of Vilna (often called the "Gra"), lived from 5480 to 5557 (1720 to 1797 C.E.). He was one of the greatest Torah scholars of the eighteenth century, and his diligence in learning was unparalleled.

From a young age, the Vilna Gaon would learn Torah twenty-two hours a day.

He knew the entire Torah by heart. He would review the entire *Talmud Bavli* every month (*Peas HaShulchan*).

He had about seven leading disciples, including Rabbi Chaim Volozhiner, to whom he bequeathed his method of learning and his many great insights.

Seeking to improve his character perfection, he wrote to the Dubno Maggid, asking him to come and inspire him with his parables.

The Chazon Ish, Rabbi Avraham Yeshayah Karelitz writes (Letter 32): "We consider the Vilna Gaon as part of the chain of transmission of Torah from Moshe Rabbeinu through Ezra, Rabbeinu HaKadosh, Rav Ashi, Rambam.... He is considered as one of the *rishonim*...."

Rabbi Chaim Volozhiner said that although his brother, Rabbi Zalman of Volozhin, also knew the entire Torah by heart, it would take Rabbi Zalman a thousand years to achieve even a small amount of the Gaon's wisdom!

After the Vilna Gaon's death, his students published many of his teachings.

*   *   *

Rabbi Chaim Volozhiner, the chief disciple of the Vilna Gaon, lived from 5509 to 5581 (1749 to 1821 C.E.).

He founded the great yeshivah in Volozhin, Lithuania, in 1803 C.E., and taught the Vilna Gaon's method of learning to hundreds of disciples. The yeshivah movement of today is a direct result of Rabbi Chaim's yeshivah.

Rabbi Chaim wrote two important *sefarim*, *Ruach Chaim* on *Avos* and *Nefesh HaChaim*, work of *hashkafah*. In *Nefesh HaChaim*, he teaches the marvelous *segulah* (method) of protecting oneself from danger: to focus on the reality that Hashem is the One Controller of everything — there is no other force besides Him.

One-minute history lesson: At intervals throughout history, Hashem provides us with super spiritual giants, leaders who are equal to those of earlier generations who broaden our horizons and help us to reach greater heights. The Vilna Gaon was such a leader. In his commentary to *Mishlei* (4:13), he teaches that the primary purpose of life is perfection of character. This idea crystallizes our life's purpose.

Chapter 71

Three Scholars of the Nineteenth Century

Rabbi Akiva Eiger, one of the leaders of his generation, lived from 5521 to 5597 (1761 to 1837 C.E.). He wrote several deep *sefarim* of halachah; *chiddushei Torah* (novel insights); and glosses on the Mishnah, Gemara, and *Shulchan Aruch*.

His greatness in Torah was matched by his tremendous humility. When people wrote him letters and addressed him with glorious titles, he would skip that portion of the letter.

He once filled in a missing page in a Rashba (see chapter 60) from memory.

He studied Torah with such enthusiasm that he never forgot his learning (*Chut HaMeshulash*, p. 177).

In the preface to his *Responsa*, he writes that at times he elaborated on the details of the questions

presented because he knew that the person present-
ing the question was suffering and he was attempting to cheer him up.

He wrote that his wife was exceptionally righteous and modest and that many times they would
have discussions in Torah matters until midnight
(*Chut HaMeshulash*, p. 65).

He wrote himself a poem in the order of the *alef-
beis* to remind himself of his purpose and goals in
life. The following is a brief summary of the poem:

א - *Prepare provisions before your time is up,*

ב -*Before your lights go out.*

ג - *Repair your deficits before you leave.*

ד - *Be aware of Hashem.*

ה - *Your body will be returned to the earth,*
to a dark grave,

ו - *Remember the day you will be leaving.*

ז - *Your wealth will go to others,*

ח - *Your heirs will appreciate their inheritance.*

ט - *Your descendants will remember you once a year.*

י - *Your friends will focus on others.*

כ - *You will be dressed in white and covered with*
black,

ל - *With some straw underneath.*

מ - *A candle at your feet toward the door,*

נ - *Surrounded by people,*

ס - *Carried by others,*

ע - *Your mouth and eyes will be closed.*

פ - *Food for the worms,*

צ - *Your relatives will return home, leaving you alone.*

ק - *Focus on this reality, and repent from your sins.*

ר - *Now is the time, before it is too late.*

ש - *Think of the Day of Judgment, and*

ת - *Keep thanking Hashem, with His help you can succeed every step of the way.*

*   *   *

Rabbi Moshe Sofer, the Chasam Sofer, lived from 5523 to 5599 (1763 to 1839 C.E.). He was known to be one of the most learned people of his generation, and he wrote many responsa which were published under the name *She'elos U'Teshuvos Chasam Sofer.*

When his first wife died, he married the daughter of Rabbi Akiva Eiger.

By age fifteen, he had completed all of *Shas.*

He was the *rav* of Pressburg, Austria, for many years. In addition, he established a yeshivah which drew hundreds of students.

For more than forty years, he did not miss even one day of teaching Torah in his yeshivah (*Derashos* 1:61).

Before each of his lectures on Talmud, he would teach a portion of *Chovos HaLevavos* for fifteen minutes.

In the preface to his responsa on *Yoreh Dei'ah*, he writes, "As long as Hashem gives me life and strength, I am prepared to learn with all those who are willing to listen, at no charge.... My writings on Torah are available to all as *hefker* [ownerless]; all may copy these lessons...."

* * *

Rabbi Samson Raphael Hirsch was a leading opponent of the Haskalah, the Enlightenment, which was beginning to spread in Germany and Austria in that time.

Rabbi Samson Raphael Hirsch lived from 5568 to 5648 (1808 to 1888 C.E.). From the time he was a young man, he fought the Reform Movement, first by writing Torah books such as *The Nineteen Letters of Ben Uziel* and *Chorev*, and later by establishing Torah schools and teaching people Torah values in person.

It was said that one who learned his book *The Nineteen Letters of Ben Uziel* would become a new person in his understanding of Torah Judaism. Rabbi Yisrael Salanter (see next chapter), the leader of the *Mussar* Movement, promoted the reading of this *sefer* and had it translated into various languages.

Rabbi Hirsch wrote many *sefarim*, including commentaries on Chumash, *Tehillim*, mitzvos, and the siddur.

One-minute history lesson: The nineteenth century saw the invention of many devices, including the telephone and the lightbulb. It is important to remember that Hashem is the One who provides people with the power and imagination to invent machines and devices. He also provides us with the ability to write *sefarim* for the Jewish nation. Each *sefer* is a form of light that illuminates the world for all time, and each Torah Sage is like a living *sefer Torah* illuminating the world for his generation and forever.

Chapter 72

Rabbi Yisrael Salanter

Rabbi Yisrael Salanter lived from 5570 to 5643 (1810 to 1883 C.E.). He is best known for establishing the *Mussar* Movement.

When he was fourteen, a selection of his *chiddushim* were sent to Rabbi Akiva Eiger (see previous chapter), who was very impressed.

Reb Yisrael observed and emulated the behavior of Rabbi Zundel of Salant and became exceptionally great. One of the pivotal lessons from Reb Zundel was: "Learn *mussar* [ethical teachings] to know how to serve Hashem."

He inspired people all over Eastern Europe to study more Torah and *mussar* and founded study groups that learned *Mesilas Yesharim*, *Orchos Tzaddikim*, and *Chayei Adam*. He also started a journal that printed insights of Torah and *mussar*.

Rabbi Aharon Kotler, *zt"l* (see chapter 76), once met an individual who was heavily involved in the establishment of many yeshivos. Rav Kotler asked the man, "Who inspired you to be so ambitious in this area?" The man replied that he once saw Rabbi Yisrael Salanter and that encounter inspired him to devote himself to spreading Torah all over.

Reb Yisrael's primary goals in life were to spread the study of Torah, *mussar*, and *middos* improvement (*Or Yisrael*). For a while he was a *rosh yeshivah* in Vilna, but when he realized that another Torah leader in town was losing students because they were going to Reb Yisrael, he stopped teaching. A collection of his letters and teachings were published by his disciple, Rabbi Yitzchak Blazer, in the *sefer Or Yisrael*.

Mussar teaches us to develop our awareness of Hashem until it penetrates to the core of our being and governs all our actions. Some of the principles of *mussar* are summed up in the thirteen character traits taught in the *sefer Cheshbon HaNefesh*, which Reb Yisrael promoted. They are 1) truth, 2) alacrity (*zerizus*), 3) diligence, 4) respect for others, 5) tranquility (*menuchas hanefesh*), 6) gentleness, 7) cleanliness, 8) patience, 9) organization, 10) humility, 11) justice, 12) thriftiness, and 13) silence.

One-minute history lesson: Reb Yisrael once saw a candle burning late at night. Upon inquiry, he learned that the source of the candle was the town tailor. Reb Yisrael asked the tailor why he was working so late. The tailor replied,

"As long as the candle burns, there is still time to make repairs." Reb Yisrael was impressed with this seemingly simple sentence and applied it to the spiritual realm of his own life and to that of all others in his generation.

Chapter 73

More Contributions to the Torah World

Rabbi Shlomo Ganzfried lived from 5564 to 5646 (1804 to 1886 C.E.). Rabbi Ganzfried realized that the average person of his day was in need of a short, accurate summary of all the halachos. He therefore wrote the *Kitzur Shulchan Aruch* (the "concise *Shulchan Aruch*"), which is still studied in our day.

The Chasam Sofer (see chapter 71) in his Responsa to *Yoreh Dei'ah* (ch. 137) praises Rav Ganzfried greatly.

His first *sefer* was *Keses HaSofer*, covering the laws applicable to scribes. The Chasam Sofer, in his approbation to this *sefer*, writes that a scribe must be well versed in this *sefer* in order to qualify for work in this field.

*   *   *

The Ben Ish Chai, Rabbi Yosef Chaim, lived from 5592 to 5669 (1832 to 1909). He was the rabbi of Baghdad for fifty years and was known as a great Torah scholar and Kabbalist. He spoke every Shabbos afternoon for three hours on the parashah and on halachic topics that he connected to the parashah. This became his famous work, *Ben Ish Chai*. He wrote many *sefarim* and answered many halachic questions from all over the world. His *sefarim* are still studied today.

*   *   *

The Sefas Emes, Rabbi Yehudah Leib Alter of Ger, lived from 5607 to 5665 (1847 to 1905 C.E.). He was the grandson of the Chiddushei HaRim, the Gerer Rebbe, and succeeded his grandfather as rebbe.

The Sefas Emes was an illustrious *talmid chacham* and leader of Polish Jewry. He wrote commentaries on *Tehillim, Koheles, Mishlei, Esther, Pirkei Avos*, and Gemara. They were given the name *Sefas Emes* after his passing because of a verse in *Mishlei* containing these words, with which he ended his commentary on the Torah and *yamim tovim*.

*   *   *

Rabbi Yosef Dov Soloveitchik lived from 5580 to 5652 (1820 to 1892 C.E.). He is known as the "Beis HaLevi" after the title of the *sefarim* that he wrote on Chumash and halachah.

In the preface to his *sefer* on Chumash, the Beis

HaLevi writes that he does not mind if speakers use his material even without giving him credit.

*   *   *

Rabbi Yosef Dov's son, Rabbi Chaim Soloveitchik, lived from 5613 to 5678 (1853 to 1918 C.E.). He is known as "Reb Chaim Brisker" after the town where he and his father served as *rav*.

Reb Chaim's system of analyzing the Talmud and Rambam has been taught to thousands of disciples and has spread throughout the world. His son, Rabbi Yitzchak Zev Soloveitchik, writes in his introduction to Reb Chaim's *sefer* on the Rambam that Hashem sent Reb Chaim to illuminate our generation's eyes in Torah and to instruct us on how to learn the *rishonim*.

He trained himself to always keep his mind on his learning, even while involved in worldly matters and the needs of the community.

In addition to being a great genius in learning, he was involved in countless forms of *chesed*.

One-minute history lesson: One of the biggest contributors to the Torah world at this time was a woman named Sarah Schenirer, who began the first network of Torah schools for girls, Bais Yaakov. Rabbi Yechezkel Sarna is quoted saying that this woman did more for the Jewish nation in the last hundred years than anyone else did. How did she merit this?

He explains that it was because she was willing to cry for the Jewish girls who were being lost to *klal Yisrael*. Her crying helped her merit to do more for them and save them.

If we cry for the various needs of the Jewish people, we will merit to contribute to Jewish history.

Chapter 74

Two Great Mussar Masters

Rabbi Simchah Zissel Broide, known as the Alter of Kelm, lived from 5584 to 5658 (1824 to 1898 C.E.). He was one of the three main disciples of Rabbi Yisrael Salanter (see chapter 72), who praised him greatly.

His yeshivah in Kelm was famous for its high scholastic standards and for its approach to *mussar* and character training.

Reb Simchah Zissel taught that the study of *mussar* is essential for a person to reach greatness. One of the main components of *mussar* is insightful thinking.

Reb Simchah Zissel also taught that order and self-discipline are vital for achieving perfection. Being punctual is a cardinal trait for developing one's character. If one behaves in a careless and untidy manner, his mind becomes confused and disorganized as well.

Reb Simchah Zissel's disciples include Rabbi Nassan Tzvi Finkel, the Alter of Slabodka; Rabbi Yerucham Levovitz, who was *mashgiach* of the Mir Yeshivah; and Rabbi Yechezkel Levenstein, of both the Mir and Ponevezhe yeshivos.

*   *   *

Rabbi Nassan Tzvi Finkel lived from 5609 to 5687 (1849 to 1927 C.E.). He was called the Alter of Slabodka because he began and led the Slabodka Yeshivah.

Rabbi Nassan Tzvi Finkel was exceptional in his wisdom and humility and in his expertise in developing the potential of his disciples. Many of today's greatest yeshivos are offshoots of his yeshivah in Slabodka.

In his lectures, he focused on the sublime greatness of people.

One-minute history lesson: The Mishnah in *Avos* (2:11) enumerates in brief the praises of the five greatest disciples of Rabbi Yochanan ben Zakai. Why does this qualify as a *mishnah* in *Shas*?

Every disciple has unique strong points that the Rebbe has to learn in order to teach him effectively. One cannot teach a disciple who has perfect recall the same way one would teach a creative genius. Like the Alter of Slabodka, we must each strive to pinpoint what makes a person tick and help him develop that potential.

Train a person according to his way so that as he matures he will not stray from it.
(*Mishlei* 22:6)

Chapter 75

Prewar Giants

Rabbi Yisrael Meir HaKohen Kagan, the Chafetz Chaim, lived from 5598 to 5693 (1838 to 1933 C.E.). One of the leaders of Jewry before World War II, he was a great tzaddik and Torah giant.

The Chafetz Chaim wrote many *sefarim* covering every possible topic and need. Rabbi Chaim Ozer Grodzensky said that the Chafetz Chaim's Torah teachings were a gift from Heaven like the *mann* in the desert: beneficial and enjoyable to all, each at his or her own level.

As an example, in his *sefer Ahavas Chesed*, the Chafetz Chaim recommends doing *chesed* for others in order to merit having children. The logic is that when you help others live, Hashem will do the same for you, measure for measure.

The Chazon Ish (*Iggros* 2:41) lists the Chafetz Chaim's *Mishnah Berurah* (a commentary on the *Shulchan Aruch*, *Orach Chaim*, divided into six volumes) as one of the nationally accepted transmissions of Torah, in line with the *Beis Yosef* (see chapter 64) and the *Magen Avraham* (see chapter 67).

*   *   *

Rabbi Chaim Ozer Grodzensky lived from 5623 to 5700 (1863 to 1940 C.E.). He was the rabbi of Vilna for many years and an important Torah leader in prewar Europe.

In the introduction to his *sefer Achiezer*, he wrote how, even in the worst of times (the time leading up to the Holocaust), he and his colleagues were still immersed in Torah study in Vilna and that the Torah was their strength and protection.

He also wrote that it was his greatest pleasure in life to help others, especially widows, orphans, the needy, and Torah scholars. He would take care of everything, for anyone in need. He would spend his days listening to people's problems and doing his best to help them (*Achiezer*, Letters 111).

One-minute history lesson: Although the Chafetz Chaim wrote many *sefarim*, his first *sefer* and the one that gave him his name was the *Chafetz Chaim*, on the laws of proper speech. The term *"chafetz chaim"* comes from *Tehillim* (34:13–14): "Who desires life (*hachafetz chaim*) and loves days to see good? Guard your tongue from evil and your lips from speaking deceitfully."

The laws on this subject are many and detailed. It is to our benefit and the benefit of others that we learn them every day. When we show Hashem that we are eager to live to the point that we study the laws on how to live successfully, it brings us a great merit for longevity.

Chapter 76

Postwar Giants

Rabbi Avraham Yeshayah Karelitz, the Chazon Ish (*ish* is based on an acronym of his name, and *chazon* means "vision of"), lived from 5639 to 5714 (1879 to 1954 C.E.). From 1933 on, he lived in Bnei Brak, Israel, from where he guided world Jewry.

From the day of his bar mitzvah, he committed himself to study Torah for its own sake with all his energy.

He was exceptionally humble and great, and he wrote *sefarim* on every topic. In addition, he was a genius in dealing with people from all over the world, in answering their questions and guiding them to success in life.

Numerous books were written about this Torah giant.

*   *   *

Rabbi Aharon Kotler lived from 5652 to 5722 (1892 to 1962 C.E.). He founded Beis Medrash

Govoha in Lakewood, New Jersey, a center for Torah study *lishmah* (for its own sake), which has become one of the largest and greatest yeshivos in the world today.

By the age of six, he was fluent in all twenty-four books of Tanach.

When he was sixteen, he met Reb Chaim Brisker, who said, "In the future, the whole world will rest on his shoulders."

Many of his *sefarim* on all topics have been published.

In his *sefer Mishnas Reb Aharon* (vol. 1), he wrote: "The survival of Torah is one of the great miracles of Providence. It is as great as the miracle of survival of Yisrael among the nations. Our history, which is unlike that of any other nation, is predicted in the Torah in prophecies that have come true precisely. We have Divine protection and a promise that the Torah will not be forgotten.

"The essence of life is spiritual growth. Torah study and mitzvah observance are the reality of life. The world exists for the study of Torah and service of Hashem."

One-minute history lesson: It pays for us to read about these Torah giants and to speak to people who knew them for the many lessons we can learn from their lives. Although neither the Chazon Ish or Reb Aharon Kotler are still alive, their *talmidim* can still teach us about their deeds. Their published works are also available, and they can guide us to heights of greatness if we learn them diligently.

Chapter 77

Three Great Recent Leaders

Rabbi Yaakov Kamenetzky lived from 5651 to 5746 (1891 to 1986 C.E.). He was a Torah leader in America for many years and was known for his sterling character and great honesty.

He went to learn in Slabodka at the age of fifteen, and gained much from the Alter, Reb Nassan Tzvi Finkel (see chapter 74).

For twenty years, from 1948 to 1968, he was *rosh yeshivah* of Torah Vodaas in Brooklyn, New York. His door was always open to anyone in need, and he was always available by telephone as well.

In his *sefer Emes L'Yaakov*, he asks why the Torah (*Bereishis* 23:1) emphasizes how long Sarah lived by stating: "Sarah lived one hundred years, and twenty years and seven years." He answers that this teaches us that those were the years that Hashem granted

Sarah. The news of the *akeidah*, which seemed to have caused her death, did not cause Sarah to die earlier than her allotted time.

This lesson is applicable to all of history. Even seemingly chance happenings are caused by Hashem, who guides and controls all that occurs.

Many of Reb Yaakov's teachings have been published in numerous *sefarim* called *Emes LeYaakov*.

*   *   *

Rabbi Moshe Feinstein lived from 5655 to 5746 (1895 to 1986 C.E.). He was a leader of American Jewry for many years, and he is renowned for his sharp mind and deep thinking.

Reb Moshe was born on the seventh day of Adar; thus, he was named after Moshe Rabbeinu, who was born and died on that same day.

Reb Moshe was *rosh yeshivah* of Yeshiva Mesifta Tiferes Yerushalayim for fifty years. In addition, he dealt with complex halachic issues from all over the world.

He authored many volumes of *Iggros Moshe* (answers to halachic questions), *Dibros Moshe* (a commentary of *pilpul shiurim*) on *Shas*, and *Darash Moshe* (a commentary on Chumash).

*   *   *

Rabbi Yoel Teitelbaum, the Satmar Rav, lived from 5647 to 5739 (1887 to 1979 C.E.). He was the *rav* of Satmar, Romania, until the Nazis forced him to flee. He was saved miraculously, and came to America, where he built a vibrant Chassidic community.

His teachings have been published in many volumes of *Divrei Yoel* and *VaYoel Moshe* on Chumash and *hashkafah*.

The Satmar Rav was a Holocaust survivor. He writes in *Divrei Yoel* (*Parshas Vayishlach*) that Hashem saved his life by great miracles. He felt he was not worthy of such miracles, and their purpose must have been for him to help save others and rebuild Torah institutions.

> *One-minute history lesson:* The Satmar Rav teaches in *Divrei Yoel* on the *passuk* "And Yaakov remained alone" (*Bereishis* 32:25), that this is the secret of our survival. We need to isolate ourselves from evildoers like Eisav and Lavan and devote ourselves to serving Hashem. Separating ourselves from the wicked, who are against Hashem, we must recognize Hashem as the One and Only God. When Mashiach comes, the entire world will recognize the truth.

Chapter 78

Learning from History

Rabbi Avigdor Miller lived from 5668 to 5761 (1908 to 2001 C.E.). A *rav* in New York for many years, he wrote about ten books on *haskafah* (Jewish philosophy), a five-volume English commentary on *Chumash*, one volume on the siddur, and three volumes on Jewish history in English. He gave thousands of lectures, many of which were recorded and recently transcribed.

Rabbi Miller was a great scholar who sought to educate Jews of all backgrounds in our wonderful Torah. Crowds of people attended his lectures, listening eagerly to his every word. At the end of the lectures, he would accept questions on any topic.

The following are some lessons that Rabbi Miller would often reiterate:

- One should say, "I love You, Hashem" at least once a day.

- One should realize that he is in this world to prepare for the World to Come.

- Before eating, one should say, "I'm eating to have the strength to serve Hashem."

- One should thank Hashem for his buttons, reinforced buttonholes, pockets, garment linings, and countless other things from which he benefits.

- One should pray for someone else's welfare even without him knowing about it.

- When one passes a Jewish home and sees a mezuzah, he should bless the people inside.

One-minute history lesson: Rabbi Miller taught: Why did the angel who fought with Yaakov Avinu refuse to divulge his name? In each generation, the evil inclination has new guises by which he tempts us. We are constantly faced with new challenges, all by different names. Whether we face wealth, poverty, glamor, or degradation, we need to learn the lessons of Jewish history to withstand temptations and to serve Hashem properly.

As we go forward and contribute to history with our daily lives, may Hashem watch over us and help us succeed for our own sakes and for the benefit of all of *klal Yisrael.* May we merit the Redemption speedily in our days, the time when the evil inclination will be defeated and "the world will be filled with awareness of Hashem" (*Yeshayah* 11:9).

Glossary

Acharonim — The Sages who lived from approximately 5250 to 5650 (1490 to 1890).

Aggadata — Parables used by the Sages of the Gemara to teach inspirational lessons.

Akeidah — The binding of Yitzchak by his father, Avraham, on Mount Moriah (see *Bereishis* 22:1–19).

Amoraim — The Sages of the Talmud who lived after the *tannaim*.

Anshei Knesses HaGedolah — The Great Assembly of Jewish leaders. It was composed of 120 Sages, including eighty prophets.

Av Beis Din — The head of the legal system.

Aron — Literally, "closet." Here, it refers to the Ark that held the Tablets.

Avos — Literally, "fathers." Depending on the context, the term can refer to the forefathers (Avraham, Yitzchak, and Yaakov) or a collection of the teachings of our Sages.

Baal Teshuvah — Literally, "master of return;" refers to a person who has returned to the path of Torah.

Bas kol — Heavenly voice.

BeMidbar — The fourth of the Five Books of Moses (Numbers).

Beis din — Judicial court.

Beis HaMikdash — The Holy Temple.

B'ezras Hashem — With the help of Hashem.

Birkas HaMazon — Grace after Meals.

Bnei Yisrael — The Jewish people.

Berachah (pl. **Berachos**) — Blessing.

Bereishis — The first of the Five Books of Moses (Genesis).

Chavrusa — Learning partner.

Chesed — Acts of kindness.

Chiddushim — Novel insights.

Chumash — The Five Books of Moses, or the Torah.

Churban — Destruction; refers to the destruction of the First or Second Temples.

Derashah (pl. **Derashos**) — Lecture.

Devarim — The fifth of the Five Books of Moses (Deuteronomy).

Emunah — Faith in Hashem.

Eretz Yisrael — The Land of Israel.

Gemara — The commentary of the Sages on the Mishnah. See Talmud.

Gematrios — Numerical values of Hebrew letters.

Haftarah (pl. **Haftaros**) — Weekly reading from the Prophets.

Halachah — Jewish law.

Hashkafah — The Torah outlook.

Kabbalah — Jewish mysticism.

Klal Yisrael — The Jewish nation.

Kohein Gadol — High Priest.

Kesuvim — Writings (the third of the three divisions of Tanach).

Lishmah — "For its sake"; used to indicate pure motives in doing a mitzvah, i.e., doing it because it is the command of Hashem.

Mann — The manna, the miracle food which the Jewish nation ate in the desert for forty years.

Masechta (pl. *Masechtos*) — Tractate, volume.

Middah keneged middah — Measure for measure.

Middos — Character traits.

Midrash (pl. *midrashim*) — A Torah lesson through a story, parable, or metaphor; a collective name for these lessons.

Mishkan — The Tabernacle.

Mishlei — The Book of Proverbs.

Mishnah — The oral law received by Moshe, set down in Six Orders.

Mizbei'ach — Altar.

Mussar — Ethical teachings.

Nach — Eight books of Prophets and eleven books of Writings.

Nasi — The spiritual leader of the Jewish people.

Navi (pl. **Nevi'im**) — A prophet. Also used to refer to the portion of Tanach that records their messages.

Parashah — The weekly Torah portion.

Pilpul — A method or style of studying the Gemara with analysis and sharp insights.

Pirkei Avos — Ethical teachings from the Sages.

Passuk (pl **Pesukim**) — A sentence or phrase of Tanach.

Peshat — Literal explanation of a verse in Tanach.

Responsa — Replies from a recognized scholar on various religious topics. Compare *teshuvah*.

Rishonim — The Sages who lived from approximately 4349 to 4798 (589 to 1038 C.E.).

Rosh Yeshivah — Head of a yeshivah.

Ruach HaKodesh — Divine inspiration.

Sanhedrin — The assembly of seventy-one Sages headed by the *av beis din*, the head of the legal system, and the *nasi*, the leader of the Torah sages and the spokesman for the nation.

Sefer (pl. **sefarim**) — Books; here refers to Torah books.

Semichah — Rabbinical ordination.

Shabbos — The seventh day of the week, which is sanctified as a day of rest.

Shas — An acronym for the Six Orders of the Talmud formed by the Hebrew words *shishah sidrei* (Six Orders).

Shechinah — Divine presence.

Shemoneh Esrei — Literally, "eighteen"; refers to the silent prayer said three times a day, which now comprises nineteen blessings.

Shidduch — A matrimonial match.

Shemittah — Every seventh year; which is sanctified.

Shemos — The second of the Five Books of Moses (Exodus).

Siman — Chapter of a *sefer*; a sign from Hashem; or mnemonic device used to aid in memorizing lessons.

Sinas chinam — Senseless hatred of others.

Talmid chacham — Torah scholar.

Talmud — The oral law, consisting of the Mishnah, the basic information on the topic, and the Gemara, the commentary of the Sages on the topic.

Talmud Bavli — Babylonian Talmud.

Talmud Yerushalmi — Jerusalem Talmud.

Tanach — Acronym (based on the Hebrew) for Torah, Nevi'im (Prophets) and Kesuvim (Writings).

Tannaim — The Sages whose teachings of the oral tradition in the Mishnah were eventually preserved in written form. Cf. *Amoraim*.

Tehillim — Psalms, one of the twenty-four books of Tanach.

Teshuvah — Literally, "return." Often associated with repentance. It can also refer to responses to questions on halachic issues. Compare Responsa.

Tishah B'Av — The ninth day of the Jewish month of Av, on which many tragic events in Jewish history happened.

Tosefta — Teachings of the Sages not included in the Mishnah.

Tzaddik — A righteous person.

Vayikra — The third of the Five Books of Moses (Leviticus).

Yetzer hara — The evil inclination.

Yetzer tov — The good inclination.

Bibliography

Chasidah, Yishai. *Encyclopedia of Biblical Personalities*. New York: Shaar Press, 1994.

Fendel, Rabbi Zechariah. Series of Hashkafah History Books. New York: Hashkafo Publications.

Finkel, Rabbi A. Y. *Great Torah Commentators*. Jason Aronson Publications, 1990.

Goldwurm, Rabbi Hersh. The *Rishonim*. New York: ArtScroll/Mesorah Publications, 1982.

Kantor, R. M. *The Jewish Time Line Encyclopedia*. Jason Aronson Publications, 1992.

Miller, Rabbi Avigdor. *Behold a People*. New York, 5728 (1968).

Miller, Rabbi Avigdor. *Exalted People*. New York, 5744 (1984).

Miller, Rabbi Avigdor. *Torah Nation*. New York, 5731 (1971).

Rotenberg, Rabbi Shlomo. *Am Olam: The History of the Eternal Nation*, Volumes I and II. Jerusalem: Feldheim Publishers, 1988.

Stern, Rabbi Y. M. *Gedolei HaDoros*, Volumes I, II, and III.

Jerushalmi Machon Minchas Yisrael, 5756 (1996).

Stone Edition of Tanach. New York: ArtScroll/Mesorah Publications, 2001.

Wein, Rabbi Berel. *Echoes of Glory: The Story of the Jews in the Classical Era, 350 BCE –750 BC*. New York: Shaar Press, 1996.